CATHOLICISM IN AMERICA

INTERPRETATIONS OF AMERICAN HISTORY

★ ★ ★ JOHN HIGHAM AND BRADFORD PERKINS, EDITORS

CATHOLICISM IN AMERICA

EDITED BY
Philip Gleason
University of Notre Dame

HARPER & ROW, PUBLISHERS
NEW YORK, EVANSTON, AND LONDON

Library of Congress Catalog Card Number: 74-121629

CONTENTS

EDITORS' INTRODUCTION

This volume—and companions in the series, "Interpretations of American History"—makes a special effort to cope with one of the basic dilemmas confronting every student of history. On the one hand, historical knowledge shares a characteristic common to all appraisals of human affairs. It is partial and selective. It picks out some features and facts of a situation while ignoring others that may be equally pertinent. The more selective an interpretation is, the more memorable and widely applicable it can be. On the other hand, history has to provide what nothing else does: a total estimate, a multifaceted synthesis, of man's experience in particular times and places. To study history, therefore, is to strive simultaneously for a clear, selective focus and for an integrated, over-all view.

In that spirit, each volume of the series aims to resolve the varied literature on a major topic or event into a meaningful whole. One interpretation, we believe, does not deserve as much of a student's attention as another simply because they are in conflict. Instead of contriving a balance between opposing views, or choosing polemical material simply to create an appearance of controversy, Professor Gleason has exercised his own judgment on the relative importance of different aspects or interpretations of a problem. We have asked him to select some of what he considers the best, most persuasive writings bearing on Catholicism in America, indicating in the introductory essay and headnotes his reasons for considering these accounts convincing or significant. When appropriate, he has also brought out the relation between older and more recent approaches to the subject. The editor's own competence and experience in the field enable him to provide a sense of order and to indicate the evolution and complexity of interpretations. He is, then, like other editors in this series, an informed participant rather than a mere observer, a student sharing with other students the results of his own investigations of the literature on a crucial phase of American development.

JOHN HIGHAM
BRADFORD PERKINS

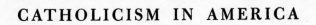

CATHOLICISM IN AMERICA

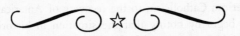

INTRODUCTION

In 1964 Henry F. May wrote in the *American Historical Review* that the "recovery of American religious history" might well be the most important achievement in the study of American culture in the last thirty years. After sketching the ways in which the investigation of religious phenomena by scholars like F. O. Matthiessen, Perry Miller, H. Richard Niebuhr, Arthur M. Schlesinger, Sr., and Ralph H. Gabriel has deepened our understanding of the national past, May went on to say that Roman Catholics were one of the two groups (the other being atheists) who had contributed least to this enterprise. Jewish historians, he noted, were much more successful in dealing with "exactly the problem so difficult for Catholics: the adjustment of an old and international religion to a Protestant or post-Protestant national culture." Such a verdict coming from Professor May cannot be disregarded since he is a leading intellectual historian whose reputation was established twenty years ago by a work in religious history, *The Protestant Churches and Industrial America.* Nor would many Catholic historians wish to dispute his judgment, although it is hoped this volume will show that there is a growing body of scholarship addressing itself to the relationship between Catholicism and American society and culture.

In attempting to account for the meagre contribution made by students of American Catholicism to the recovery of American religious history we may begin by noting that the situation in historical scholarship is part of the larger picture of Catholic inadequacy in the intellectual sphere about which so much was written after John Tracy Ellis's famous critique in 1955 (reprinted in this volume). The causal factors reviewed by the critics of the Catholic intellectual record—immigrant background, lower-class status, lack of an intellectual tradition, weak achievement orientation, ghetto mentality, clerical paternalism, authoritarianism, and so on—all presumably have something to do with inhibiting the work of Catholic historians.

The "ghetto" situation of Catholics is perhaps especially relevant because it affected not only Catholic historians but also students of general American history. Catholics were, as the cliché has it, not in "the mainstream." They regarded themselves and were regarded by others as being somehow off to themselves, occupied by concerns that were not of great moment to anybody else and still less of vital importance to American national development. Catholics were not the original founders or influential shapers of the national culture. Claims that their participation was crucial to American victory in the War for Independence, or that Thomas Jefferson's ideas were derived from the sixteenth-century Jesuit theologian, Robert Bellarmine, were properly dismissed as exaggerations. Although *in* the national story, Catholics seemed so little part *of* it that historians who consider the matter at all are even yet troubled as to how Catholic history is to be integrated into the pattern of national development. Since few historians wish to devote their energies to matters universally deemed peripheral, the history of Catholicism until very recent times attracted no attention from students of the general history of the United States. And reluctance to enter a field that seems parochial is still observable among graduate students at Catholic universities.

The growth of social history in the twentieth century stimulated interest in religious history, with Arthur Schlesinger at Harvard guiding a number of students into the field. The work of two of Schlesinger's disciples is of special interest. The first, Ray Allen Billington, contributed in his *Protestant Crusade* (1938) the first major scholarly work on Catholic history written by a general American historian who was not a Catholic. It is notable, however, that Catholics are cast as passive victims in this history of nativism before the Civil War. So far from being founders or shapers of the nation, Catholics were seen as the outsiders, the enemies. In the colonial era the Catholic Spanish and French beyond the borders of English settlement were the chief religious and political enemies; in the nineteenth century Catholics became a sizeable element in the growing American population, but they were still feared as a hostile group threatening the integrity of the republic. For the progressive-minded historian interested in the social evolution of the American people, the aspect of Catholic history most attractive was how Catholics had been received by the host society. Later work by historians of immigration, notably Carl Wittke and Oscar Handlin and his students, carried this approach further. The principal integration of Catholic history with the general development of the nation has, therefore, been through the study of the reception and adjustment of Catholic newcomers to an often inhospitable society. But it is noteworthy that Billington who pioneered in this approach among non-Catholic historians did no further work in Catholic history after publishing the book that grew out of Schlesinger's seminar. Instead he turned to a subject more in the mainstream, the story of westward expansion and the frontier.

The second of Schlesinger's students whose career is instructive is Aaron I. Abell. A midwesterner from rural Illinois, Abell was a Catholic who traced his origins back to the early English Catholic group in Maryland, many of whom followed the trans-Appalachian migration into central Kentucky. Although he became the leading authority on Catholic social action in the United States, Professor Abell, who died in 1965, launched his career with a study of *The Urban Impact on American Protestantism* (1943). Thus even a leading Catholic scholar with deep American roots, guided by the foremost practitioner of social history, entered the field of religious history through what might be called the main gate of Protestantism before setting off for the Catholics out in the back forty.

But if general historians of the United States showed scant interest in Catholicism and found it difficult to relate to the dominant motifs in American history, it must also be said that they got very little help from Catholic scholars. Part of the problem was simply that Catholics were late in getting started in professional historical scholarship in the United States. Until after World War II, there was no graduate program in history worth mentioning at any Catholic institution except the Catholic

University of America. And although conscientious and scholarly workers were active in the field long before, it was only in 1915 that Peter Guilday inaugurated systematic professional training in church history at the Catholic University of America. Guilday also played a leading role in founding the *Catholic Historical Review* in 1915; four years later he spearheaded the organization of the American Catholic Historical Association. From that date until his health broke in the early 1940s, Guilday was the inspiration and driving force behind a program in American Catholic history which turned out dozens of published monographs. His successor, John Tracy Ellis, continued the tradition and maintained the Catholic University's leadership in the field through the 1940s and 1950s, although by that time other Catholic universities were developing graduate programs and individual scholars in secular universities were beginning to write on Catholic topics.

Nearly all of the students trained by Guilday, Ellis, and their Catholic University colleague, Richard J. Purcell, were priests or nuns. Although several of them continued to be productive scholars after completing their dissertations, most of these students were drawn away from research by heavy teaching and administrative responsibilities. The same was true of clerics who received their training elsewhere; and since few lay people showed much interest in Catholic history, this institutional consideration in part explains why Catholic historians contributed so little to the recovery of American religious history.

Something else adding to the problems of integrating Catholic history into the overall story of American religious development was the view of the Church held by Catholic writers. Until quite recently, Catholics ordinarily thought of the Church as a well-defined entity whose life was self-contained and essentially unchanging. Although it was recognized that the Church acted upon the world, and was acted upon by it, Catholic history written in the context of this sort of ecclesiology tended to concentrate on the Church itself rather than on the interaction of Church and surrounding society. This kind of history was of interest to Catholics because they accepted the importance of the Church, in and of itself; but it had little appeal to those who were not Catholic—which in the United States meant most people, and in the historical profession nearly everybody. In the 1960s, however, a new way of looking at the Church has gained acceptance among Catholic theologians. Official statements by the Second

Vatican Council endorsed the new ecclesiology, and a shift in thinking on the nature of the Church is rapidly filtering out into the masses of Catholics and will inevitably color the approach of historians in the future.

The fundamental emphasis of the new ecclesiology is summed up in the expression "the People of God"—a term that has almost become a shibboleth among liberal American Catholics in the last four or five years. Thinking of the Church as the People of God shifts attention away from the tangible ecclesiastical organization and brings to the forefront of consciousness the fact that the Church is also a mystical union, a spiritual fellowship made up of those who accept Jesus Christ as Master and seek to follow Him. While not denying the reality and necessity of the visible, structured Church, theologians of the new ecclesiology insist that that is not all there is to the Church. And since the older conception laid a disportionate emphasis on the formal hierarchical structure, they seek to restore the proper balance between the visible and invisible elements by reaffirming that the Church is also a spiritual community; a people called by God to work for the coming of His Kingdom.

In popular discussions, where the nuances drop away, the Church as the People of God is flatly contrasted to "the institutional Church," which is said by the more enthusiastic writers of letters to liberal Catholic publications to be "finished" or, at the very least, "outdated." These writers generally use the term to mean the juridical structure, but the institutional Church in the broadest sense is the system of beliefs and doctrines, the forms of worship, the moral code, the patterns of authority, and the rules that govern ecclesiastical administration and organizational interaction—everything, in summary, that pertains to the Church as a formal institution.

Since the Middle Ages, and especially since the sixteenth-century Council of Trent, the Catholic Church has undergone a tremendous process of institutional elaboration. Included in this process were the definition and specification of doctrine, the systematization of clerical education, the centralization of ecclesiastical government, the codification of canon law, and in the United States the burgeoning of ancillary agencies such as schools, hospitals, and church-related societies. As this ecclesiastical exoskeleton took on proportions of baroque magnificence and intricacy, Catholics tended to think of it as the Church, total and complete, than which there was nothing more. For the average American Catholic this did not mean that the Church seemed impersonal or bureaucratic. On the contrary, the expression "Holy Mother Church" spoke to the depths of the Catholic heart. But while the Church was intimate and personal, it was still somehow external—something to which the Catholic adhered, rather than something which he and his fellow believers constituted by their shared faith in the presence of God among them.

The historiographical implications of this view of the Church are obvious. Religious concerns of surpassing importance were bound up with a Church that existed as a visible reality with definite boundaries. Geographically considered, the Church was a network of ecclesiastical units called dioceses. To write the history of one of these units was to record the past life of the Church in its local embodiment. To trace the expansion of diocesan jurisdictions was to tell the story of the Church's growth. Those who filled the administrative slots of the hierarchical structure were important by that fact alone. Hence biographies of bishops loom large in the writings of American Catholic historians, and the lives of distinguished prelates like John Carroll, the first American bishop, or Cardinal James Gibbons, serve as focal points for the exposition of Catholic development in their epochs. Much of the span of Catholic history in the United States is therefore woven into a sort of "episcopal synthesis." And since official records were retained in chanceries and bishops often saved their correspondence, the institutional Church not only threw up well-defined subjects for historical study it also automatically generated the sources necessary for such study. The ancillary institutions such as religious communities and colleges likewise afforded natural subjects and materials for historians.

Historical investigations guided by the older conception of the Church thus had the advantages of clarity of subject matter and relative abundance and accessibility of sources. Nor could one deny that works employing this approach are a legitimate and valuable kind of Catholic history. If the Church is really to be said to exist in the world it must take on concrete form, embody itself in identifiable structures, and mobilize the energies of real people who perform various functions related to its activities. All of these offer objects of historical study; and great history has been written from the perspective of the older ecclesiology. John Gilmary Shea, whose four-volume *History of the Catholic Church in the United States* (1886-1892) has never been superseded, worked entirely within the context of that ecclesiology. As Henry Warner Bowden has recently pointed out, Shea "viewed the Church as coterminous with the duly consecrated hierarchy and activities sanctioned by them . . ."

But Shea's perspective put very narrow limits on what could properly be conceived as Catholic history. Narrowness was the most serious drawback of the older approach, but it was not the only one. This sort of history tended to be annalistic and was difficult to synthesize except through the biographical "great bishops" device. Moreover, it usually concentrated heavily on the internal development of ecclesiastical institutions and neglected analysis of the interaction between the Church and the surrounding social milieu. As a result, the story of American Catholicism existed in a sort of historical vacuum. As Catholic historians absorb the contemporary ecclesiology it is reasonable to hope that these shortcomings will be corrected, for the People of God concept of the Church is closely linked with greater emphasis on the layman and his role in bringing the witness of a "Servant Church" to bear in the modern world.

It would be misleading to suggest, however, that historians of American Catholicism have altogether overlooked the laity in their preoccupation with institutional history. Long before the expression "People of God" came in vogue, historians opened up several avenues of investigation dealing with the vicissitudes of Catholics considered as a subgroup within American society. Nativism furnished the earliest major focus of Catholic commentary and scholarship on the general theme of adjustment to American circumstances. Catholic involvement in the problems of labor and social reform has also received a good deal of attention. Consideration of Catholics as immigrants was necessarily entailed in these topics and other studies dealt directly with the fortunes of various Catholic ethnic groups. In the 1940s the late Thomas T. McAvoy, C.S.C., sketched a general interpretation of Catholics as a minority in American society; ten years later he devoted a volume to a key episode in the late nineteenth century in which the relationship of Catholicism to American culture was disputed both on the level of social policy and that of theological understanding. And in 1958 the non-Catholic scholar, Robert D. Cross, published a broad-ranging study of the emergence of an American-style liberalism among Catholics in the United States.

These studies antedated widespread acquaintance with the People of God concept of the Church, but it might be argued that they pointed in the direction of the new ecclesiology. However that may be, it is a virtual certainty that a different understanding of what the Church is will eventually make itself felt in the work of Catholic historians. It would be hazardous to predict just how the new ecclesiological influence will shape future historical studies. At present, it seems to me, the implications are uncertain because the concept itself is still imperfectly grasped—at least among non-theologians. As the expression "People of God" is used in popular discussions it often blurs the boundaries between Church and world, and one sometimes gets the impression that whatever Catholics— or Christians, or men of good will—do, they are to be understood as doing it as the People of God, and hence they are the Church in action. If this view should prevail, it would be difficult to distinguish between religion and everything else, and the Church would tend to disappear as a distinct object of historical study. This is, of course, an extreme possibility, but it might be the case that a loss of precision will be the price exacted for greater comprehensiveness in Catholic history. But the precision of the older history was also bought at a price. And if the new ecclesiology stimulates historians of American Catholicism to cast a wider net in their researches, the results ought surely to contribute more significantly to the recovery of American religious history.

The essays in this volume deal with the relationship of Catholicism to American society and culture. Most of them were written in the 1960s, but none attempts to apply the new ecclesiology as an interpretive framework in the analysis of the events, movements, or institutions with which they are concerned. Hence they may be thought of as exemplifying the emergence of a broader interest in lay activities and in the interaction of Catholics and American society within the context of the older conception of the Church.

The volume opens with an essay of McAvoy's first published in 1948. It is probably the most widely read of his articles dealing with the history of the "Catholic minority" and illustrates his interest in the interaction between the Catholic tradition and the American tradition. The next selection by James Hennesey, S.J., also examines this interaction and is centered on roughly the same time period studied by McAvoy. Hennesey's focus is different, however, since he is primarily concerned with the impact of the American experience on official Catholic church policy and thinking. The third essay is a study of an important clash over education, and the next two articles take up aspects of the adjustment of the two most important Catholic immigrant groups in the nineteenth century, the Irish and the Germans.

The last five selections proceed chronologically from the Progressive era to the 1960s. In Kenneally's and Cuddy's articles we see something of the complexity of Catholic reactions to issues of domestic politics and foreign affairs in the first two decades of this century. The next article returns to the question of Catholics and social reform, and explicitly relates Catholic attitudes on social issues to the theme of Americanism. The last two essays reflect the concerns of the decades in which they were written. Monsignor Ellis' essay on Catholic intellectual life is a landmark in American Catholic self-understanding and was recognized as such from its publication in 1955. The final selection, by the editor of this volume, uses a theoretical framework derived from the study of immigrant groups in interpreting the situation of American Catholicism in the 1960s.

The Formation of
the Catholic Minority

THOMAS T. McAVOY, C.S.C.

Americanization is the great theme in the history of the Catholic Church in the United States. Catholic historians have become increasingly engaged by this theme in recent years; none has done more to stimulate its study than Thomas T. McAvoy, C.S.C. Father McAvoy, Archivist at the University of Notre Dame for forty years and Head of Notre Dame's History Department from 1939 to 1960, had an unmatched knowledge of the manuscript sources of American Catholic history. His death in July, 1969, removed one of the great modern scholars from this field. He was the author of several books, of which the most important is *The Great Crisis in American Catholic History* (1957), but he may be remembered longest for essays outlining an original perspective on the development of Catholicism in the United States. McAvoy approached Catholic history as the story of a minority group interacting with other elements in American society; and he stressed the importance of the early Anglo-American nucleus in giving an "American" character to the Church in the United States. The article reprinted here is the most widely read and influential statement of his thesis.

N O MINORITY GROUP IN THE UNITED STATES IS PROBABLY AS formless and yet at the same time as rigid as the American membership of the Roman Catholic Church. The rigidity of the Catholic organization arises from the fact that there has never been a real heresy during the three centuries and more of Catholic life within the

Thomas T. McAvoy, C.S.C., "The Formation of the Catholic Minority in the United States 1820-1860," *The Review of Politics,* X (January, 1948), 13-34. Reprinted without footnotes by permission of the publishers.

boundaries of the present United States. Even the so-called heresy of Americanism existed more in the minds of European theologians than in the Catholics of the new world. There have been divergencies among American Catholics on such questions as the application of Gregory XVI's condemnation of the slave trade, the timeliness of the declaration of papal infallibility or the extent of the papal condemnation of secret societies but there has been no difference on the essential doctrines involved in these disputes. In startling contrast to this unity in dogma and morals has been the extreme divergence among American Catholics in political beliefs and in economic and social status. What there is of a distinctive Catholic culture is the result of the interaction between the doctrinal unity and this political, social and economic divergence. It took its dominant form during the stormy years immediately before the Civil War.

• • •

Roughly, all American cultural ideals are compounded of two elements, the European traditions brought by the immigrant and the effects of the American frontier—in a broad sense of the term—on these immigrants. American Catholic culture has been no exception to the process but the Catholic minority history differs from the history of the majority Protestant group because the Catholic immigrants have been overwhelmingly non-English. American Catholic culture has undergone a series of rises and declines under the effect of successive waves of non-English migrations and has not completely solved the problems of its later immigrants even today. Yet, the essential characteristics of American Catholic culture were determined by the generation of Catholics in America during the great immigration from 1830 to the Civil War. Unwittingly the nativistic and anti-Catholic reaction of forties and fifties furnished the hammer and the anvil by which this distinctive Catholic cultural unity was created; and this cultural unity has slowly absorbed all the later immigrants since the Civil War.

In most of the historical accounts of the Catholic body in the United States the cultural composition of the group has been generally misunderstood. No one, for example, has explained why the cultural and social position of English-speaking Catholics before 1835 was higher than it has ever been since that time. Some writers do not recognize the existence of the group before the eighteen-thirties. Because the Catholic body achieved national importance only when the number of Catholics had been suddenly swollen by Irish and German immigration in the second quarter of the nineteenth century, most historians of American social and cultural life have tended to classify Catholicism as a foreign importation, almost out of harmony with the dominant Anglo-American culture. This is understandable, for no one can deny that the dominant American culture is actually English and Protestant, although greatly modified by the frontier and by American experience. The supposition that American culture is essentially Protestant, however, overlooks the fact that since 1636, at least, there has always been an English Catholic minority, truly Catholic and truly American according to the times, within the present United States. That minority has always accepted all the essentials of English culture while remaining loyal to their Catholic faith. The members of this Anglo-American Catholic group were never very numerous. They were scarcely thirty thousand in three million in 1790, but they were accepted as fully American, even though their faith was not approved. This Catholic minority of Maryland and Pennsylvania had absorbed many non-English Catholics even before the Revolution without changing its character, because these earlier Irish, German, and French immigrants had adopted generally the cultural standards of the English Catholics and were quite indistinguishable from them after a generation in the United States.

The number of Irish, French, and German immigrants in this Anglo-American Catholic minority prior to 1820 actually was scarcely greater in relation to the English Catholics than the non-English immigrants were in relation to the total English population of the country during this early period. The relation of the Anglo-American Catholic group towards the non-Catholic majority, on the other hand, can be described roughly as the relation of the Catholic minority in England towards the English majority, minus the legal disabilities of English Catholics. Catholics in England since the Gunpowder Plot in 1605 had ceased to hope for a corporate reunion of England with the Church of Rome. They bore as best they could the social and economic persecution which cut more deeply than the political disbarment, and saw their numbers frequently lessened—before the Oxford revival—by the usual wearing away at the edges of Catholics whose faith had weakened under the strain. Nevertheless, English Catholics remained loyal to their country as well as to their Catholic friends and sought to attain the position of a select cultured minority. American Catholics before 1820, however, had higher hopes than English Catholics because they had attained equality before the law and because they had been reenforced especially by a group of cultured French priests who had fled into exile from the persecution of the French Revolution.

A second and perhaps more important reason for the usual misinterpretation of the cultural relation between the Catholic minority and the majority group in the United States has been the insistence of certain Catholic historians, particularly John Gilmary Shea and Monsignor Peter Guilday on identifying the Irish Catholic with the Catholic minority chiefly because the more numerous Irish spoke English and had adopted the United States as their country once they had landed. Such a theory, which was apparently accepted by many Irish Catholic leaders a hundred years ago, will hold in the political sphere but culturally overlooks completely the difference between English and Irish cultural ideals in the nineteenth century. It also ignores the existence of the definite Anglo-American Catholic minority in that early period. This viewpoint too hastily considered all opposition to the Irish immigrant to be based on religious belief alone. Actually the continued existence and growth of the Anglo-American Catholic group in the larger Catholic group is the chief connecting link between the history of the Catholic immigrant and that of the native Protestant and is the basic element in our distinctive American Catholic culture.

In American ecclesiasical history of the first two decades of the nineteenth century the existence of a number of French clerical exiles and their opposition to the immigrant Irish clergyman has been a source of confusion in evaluating the Catholic group of the period. These French clergy have been accused of plotting a Gallic domination of the American Church, where they were actually defenders of the Anglo-American group against an Irish invasion. That these Irish immigrants of the day, especially among the clergy, regarded themselves as more American than the French who spoke only broken and accented English was understandable. But it must be borne in mind that in the broader American scene the French Huguenots, such as the Jays, the Faneuils, the Legarés, and the Pettigrues, and the Swiss Albert Gallatin were accepted as part of the majority group without too much objection. And the Catholic French clergymen were readily received by the Anglo-American Catholics and even by American non-Catholics because of their learning and culture. Abbé Jean Cheverus and Abbé Francis Matignon were revered by the New England Yankees who despised the Irish immigrant, and Abbé Jean Dubois in Virginia and Abbé Gabriel Richard in Michigan were accepted as honorable citizens. The sympathy of these French priests was naturally with the native Americans with whom they generally associated, especially those of some social position. The Irish on the contrary were generally antagonistic toward the English, had even lost most of the traditions of ancient Irish culture and had little social position. The French clergymen, particularly Archbishop Ambrose Maréchal of Baltimore, looked upon the Irish as just as much foreigners as themselves and wanted the control of the clergy in the hands of American clergymen. Further, his antagonism toward some of the Irish clergy was based upon several cases of clerical disobedience and misconduct. Actually, most of our knowledge of the Catholic minority at this time arises from the troubles between the French Archbishop and his Irish suffragans but these troubles are symbolic of the cultural conflict within the Catholic group of that time.

Partly, perhaps, because the Irish were the most active Catholics in the English speaking world and partly because of some ecclesiastical intrigue in Rome, the Sacred Congregation of the Propaganda had been prevailed upon to appoint several Irish bishops to the American episcopate, thus giving the new Irish immigrants spokesmen for their opinions in the government of American Catholics. Father John Connolly, O.P., of Ireland was named bishop of New York in 1815, and Fathers Henry Conwell, Patrick Kelly and John England, also from Ireland, were named to the sees of Philadelphia, Richmond and Charleston, respectively. None of these men had even been in the United States before their appointment and all had been elected without any recommendation from the American bishops. Archbishop Ambrose Maréchal of Baltimore was alarmed at this action. He had proposed American-born Benedict Fenwick for Charleston and wanted either men experienced in America or, perhaps, Englishmen appointed to the other sees. He began at once to petition the Sacred Congregation against further appointments without the consultation of the American bishops. To Maréchal the increasing Irish immigration and the growth in the number of Irish priests and bishops constituted the first threat of a real foreign domination of the American church, and he felt called upon by his position to prevent such a situation. To the Irish, however, the activities of Maréchal and the other French clergymen looked rather like an attempt at Gallic domination. The care of the Anglo-American Catholics as such and the promotion of their interests seem to have rested mostly with the French clergymen since the natives had not produced enough native priests to care for their own needs.

Bishop John England, the foremost of the new Irish clergymen, was undoubtedly an outstanding ecclesiastic possessing exceptional gifts as an orator and as a journalist. Despite the fact that he was situated in a diocese containing few Catholics and away from the other Catholic centers, he began at once to influence the whole Catholic minority. He visited other Catholic congregations along the coast and founded the first really Catholic newspaper in the United States, the *U. S. Catholic Miscellany*, in 1822 for the exposition of the Catholic faith. He so delighted Catholics and non-Catholics by his oratory as to receive countless invitations to speak to American audiences throughout the country—once speaking before the Congress of the United States. Although England had been an outstanding Irish nationalist as a clergyman and editor in Ireland, he became an honest, zealous American as soon as he arrived in this country. If he seemed extremely pro-Irish in his activities it was because he felt that the Irish were the chief Catholics in the English-speaking world, European or American, and were being attacked chiefly because of their Faith. He and his fellow Irish immigrants accepted American citizenship and considered themselves entitled to all American social privileges as well. Actually, he and his confreres from Ireland were not as much a part of the American Catholic group as the French-speaking Maréchal and the French Sulpicians of St. Mary's Seminary. In the columns of the *Miscellany* even England admitted that the Irish immigrants were not all the social equals of the older English inhabitants of the country. He had, however, no great respect for the culture of the French archbishop and his Sulpician associates who, he maintained, would never be accepted by Americans because of their foreign language and accent.

In the 1820's when England insisted that Maréchal call a provincial council to lay down rules for the trustee problems and for other difficulties, Maréchal rightly understood that he could scarcely hope to control the discussions in such an assembly against these new Irish appointees. To

England's request he answered that the disciplinary troubles were purely local and that there were no new dogmatic or moral problems needing conciliar definition. At the same time, Bishop England, noting the lack of clergymen, proposed a scheme for recruiting clerical candidates from Ireland, with special arrangements to eliminate unruly candidates. But to this proposal also, Maréchal turned a deaf ear. While Maréchal did seem to look down on the Irish clergymen, so many of whom were causing disciplinary problems in New York, Philadelphia, Norfolk, and Charleston, there is another explanation for his action besides racial and national prejudice. Not even England could deny that most of the rebellious clergymen of the day were Irish. Further, there existed in the newly arrived Irish immigrants, a confusion of Irish nationalism and Catholicism in their public utterances, notably in their newspapers. Nor was the cultural level of the Irish flock as high as the Anglo-American Catholic group. Consequently Maréchal could justly feel that to place the control of the growing Catholic body in the hands of such a group would endanger the future of the American Church. He wanted a "national clergy."

Maréchal first begged Rome to check any further European intrigue in the appointment of American bishops. He sought and finally obtained the nomination of episcopal candidates by the American hierarchy. This he hoped would prevent the appointment of bishops who would be totally unacquainted with the American scene. In his own nominations he usually recommended American or English candidates and even preferred the Irish Franciscan Maguire for the proposed see of Pittsburgh over the Frenchman Stephen Theodore Badin on one occasion. He did succeed in having the English born James Whitfield appointed his coadjutor and successor and backed Maryland born Benedict Fenwick for several sees, finally succeeding in having him named to the see of Boston. Whitfield, carrying on the tradition, was in turn succeeded by the American-born and Sulpician-trained Samuel Eccleston. Thus for another generation the archiepiscopal see remained in the possession of the Anglo-American Catholics. But the rising generation of American Catholics was dominantly Irish in numbers, especially about the ports of entry and in the mill towns. The newer bishops, nominated by the existing hierarchy, continued to be Sulpician-trained, but were becoming more and more of Irish descent. Nevertheless the cultural leaven of the Catholic congregations remained the Anglo-American group who alone had social position. They were to a great extent rural, and, even partially western, as the Bardstown group of transplanted Marylanders prospered and spread about the Middle West.

Maréchal never called a provincial assembly of the bishops, but after his death Bishop England succeeded in having Rome order the Provincial Councils of 1829 and 1833. As Maréchal had foreseen, England dominated these assemblies and spoke the mind of the hierarchy in the pastoral letters to the clergy and the laity. But England's influence was checked. Even his Charleston diocese could not support the cultural institutions he planned. Likewise other bishops found that the immigrants could not support colleges and seminaries. To make cultural matters worse for the Catholic groups even the faculty of Mount St. Mary's College, the most promising cultural institution, was sacrificed to make bishops for the expanding church.

During the decade after 1833, increasing Irish immigration continued and the French clergy were not renewed in proportionate numbers. The native and Anglo-American group were not numerous enough to supply clergy for the invading thousands. Some Belgian, German, French and Italian priests were obtained but the greater number of the new clergymen were Irish or the sons of Irish immigrants. It was a natural consequence of this large number of Irish faithful and Irish clergymen that the chief candidates for episcopal honors in the growing Catholic Church in the United States during the thirties and forties should have come from these Irish immigrants, although years of service and even training in the country were prerequisites for these promotions. Father Francis Patrick Kenrick, after twelve years in the froniter seminary of Bardstown, Kentucky, became coadjutor to Bishop Jean Dubois in New York. Father John B. Purcell had risen to the presidency of Mt. St. Mary's College before he was appointed to the western see of Cincinnati. Father John Hughes had come to the United States as a young man, had received his training in this country and served with Bishop Francis Kenrick in Philadelphia. Father Peter Richard Kenrick had served in his brother's diocese of Philadelphia before being named coadjutor to Bishop Joseph Rosati in St. Louis. The German immigration into the Ohio Valley also received recognition in 1838 in the appointment of Father John Martin Henni, the editor of the German Catholic newspaper *Wahrheitsfreund,* as the first

Bishop of Milwaukee. Father Anthony Blanc, after twelve years in Louisiana, became the bishop of the French at New Orleans. Father John Timon in the new see of Buffalo, Father Richard Vincent Whelan of Richmond and Wheeling, Father Ignatius Reynolds of Charleston, Father John J. Chanche of Natchez, and, later, Father John McGill of Richmond, together with Samuel Eccleston in Baltimore and Benedict Fenwick in Boston of the older group continued for a time to carry on the Anglo-American tradition in the American hierarchy. None of these bishops was an outstanding public man. The real leadership in the Catholic hierarchy was supplied by the more active Irish-born prelates of whom John Purcell of Cincinnati seemed nearest to being a member of the old English Catholic group, perhaps because he had more fully experienced the leveling influence of the frontier. Outside of the ports of entry he was the chief American prelate, building up a notable church organization in the Middle West, which combined the older English Catholic pioneers, remnants of the French, the numerous German immigrants and the Irish who had followed the canals and railroads into the interior of the country. But even Purcell was Irish-born.

Meanwhile, as a result of the heavy Irish and German immigration between 1830 and 1850 the Catholic group in the United States had become overwhelmingly immigrant, chiefly Irish in the eastern cities and German in the colonies in the Middle West. The violence of the nativistic reaction continued. In vain did the American Bishops Timon, McGill and Whelan seek a native American for Archbishop of Baltimore when Samuel Eccleston died in 1851. Their only candidates were Chanche and Timon and they did not compare in ability to the Irish-born prelates. Rome, at the request of most of the American bishops, named Francis Patrick Kenrick of Philadelphia to the Baltimore see. Thus, when the first Plenary Council of Baltimore was convened in 1852, the American hierarchy consisted of six foreign-born archbishops and seventeen foreign-born bishops. There were no American-born archbishops and only nine of the bishops had been born in the United States. The chief archiepiscopal sees—New York, Baltimore, Cincinnati, and St. Louis—were occupied by prelates of Irish birth. In point of fact this Irish domination represented the numerical composition of the Catholic body at this time. Of the Catholic population, those in New England and the Middle Atlantic states were almost solidly Irish and were in control of nearly all the

Catholic press. The English Catholics who had increased only by conversions and by natural growth were chiefly in the upper South although many groups of them had gone to various farming regions in the Ohio valley. The German Catholic immigrants were increasing rapidly in the north central states but because of language difficulties exerted little influence on the general Catholic body.

This change in the hierarchy to Irish domination did not imply any political maneuvers by the Irish or other foreign-born ecclesiastics. The bishops were rightly chosen from the more capable of the clergy in the field and were the nominees of the other bishops both native and foreign-born. There was already some discussion of the need of separate organizations for the German faithful, who did not speak English, but Archbishop Cajetan Bedini, the papal legate who visited the country in 1853, disapproved of such a separation. There was, however, an increase in the German bishops. Altogether, then, the change in the hierarchy actually represented in a proper way the change in the cultural and national origins of the Catholic population. The cultural unity of the Catholic minority before 1830 was gradually reestablished on the foundations of the common Faith and sacraments but while the English and native-born Catholics provided the cultural leadership, the numerical predominance of the immigrant group had changed the quality and character of the whole group.

There are few manifestations of strictly cultural character by which one can estimate the cultural accomplishments of the Catholic group of that day. Outside of a few converts there were few writers or thinkers of note. The Catholic lawyers such as Roger Taney and William Read of Maryland and the Spaldings and Elders of Kentucky were examples of the continued growth of the Anglo-American Catholic group throughout the period. It is also significant that for Catholic opinions on the great national problems of the day even the immigrants took their leadership from these border states. Brownson and other Yankee converts could complain of this but they actually preferred that leadership in most affairs to dictation from the immigrant. The oratory and the Catholic press of the eastern cities were on a much lower cultural plane and were devoted rather to political than to cultural pursuits. Numerically the Catholic population was chiefly in the ports of entry and the mill towns of the North. These northern Catholics, however, were mostly poor immigrants struggling for a livelihood in the less desirable section of the towns and buffeted by the storms of nativism. Naturally their pastors were gravely concerned with their welfare and defended them not in literary journals but in the press and from pulpit and platforms. Around New York Catholic leadership in public affairs had passed into the hands of Bishop Hughes, whose diocese became the center of most of the public controversy. Closely associated with him in this work was Bishop Kenrick in Philadelphia and Bishop Fenwick and later Bishop Fitzpatrick in Boston; but no other prelate commanded the attention of the Irish immigrant and of the American public as easily as Bishop Hughes. In him the Irish immigrant group found its cleverest and most potent expression. He sought to protect the immigrants from the nativists and to direct their efforts for their own good. He exerted this protection chiefly in the field of politics and oratory where the impoverished immigrant could best be marshalled. He saved his flock from physical persecution in the riots of 1844 but he kept them in the cities where progress and cultural development for the lower classes came hardest. In general the Catholic bishops were conspicuously absent in the movement against slavery, the temperance movement or in the other social reforms of the day. They could not concern themselves with these things as long as their flocks lacked religious care and economic security.

Considering the poverty of most of the Catholic immigrants it is easy to see that the chief burden of the Catholic clergy during the three decades before the Civil War was not to build up universities or other institutions of higher culture. They were absorbed in the immediate task of giving the sacraments and essential Catholic instruction to these impoverished immigrants and of protecting them so far as possible from the fury of the nativistic movement. That this nativism was to a great extent a religious persecution is amply proven in the controversial literature of the day. But at the same time it was a cultural reaction to the influx of immigrants. So long as the dominant cultural group was so hostile to the Church it is understandable that the defenders of the Irish immigrants were the Catholic clergy and that Bishop (Archbishop after 1850) Hughes and his fellow bishops should object to the efforts of Orestes Brownson and other native American Catholics to produce harmony between the immigrant Catholic and the nativists. Indeed, for the Irish immigrant who had fled from English oppression the combination of religious and political persecution was not new. He was not surprised to find the English descendant

in America attempting to carry on the same persecution but he did appeal
to his rights as guaranteed by American law. In his appeal to the law the
immigrant was sustained but socially and culturally there remained a
division between the immigrant and the nativist which only generations
of living together could overcome.

The native-born Catholics, including the older Irish, looked forward to
the day when the immigrant would cease to be looked upon as a foreigner.
Brownson, a militant Yankee, wanted to eliminate this distinction at once.
Archbishop Hughes objected to Brownson's reasonings because he feared
that the loss in Faith in a hasty adoption of American ways would out-
weigh any social gain.* Later on the Americanized Irish would use the
Brownson argument against the Germans, Poles, and French Canadians.
In the case of the Irish immigrant, the absence of a language difficulty did
not prevent Archbishop Hughes from realizing that there was a cultural
difference between the immigrants and the native Americans. But like
the defenders of later national groups he failed to see the advantages of
a quicker Americanization. The cultural conflict in the forties and fifties
. . . was the first great manifestation of a foreign nationalism in the American church. Culturally the policy of Hughes set back the progress of the
Irish immigrant at least a generation, as such policies have set back other
Catholic groups wherever they have manifested themselves. In some instances, it is true, the opposition to the immigrant of the earlier period
included local political feeling because the immigrant had become the
tools of politicians, and there was, also, some economic feeling manifested
by the incipient labor unions against foreign labor competition. These
latter, however, were minor items in a struggle that was mainly religious
and cultural.

Since the cultural opposition to the Irish immigrant during the second
quarter of the nineteenth century was chiefly on religious grounds, it was
to the religious advantage of the Catholic group that the clerical leaders
who defended the immigrant were men from Catholic countries where
no compromise in religious matters was the order of the day. In the
Catholic unity moulded by the nativistic opposition, American Catholi-

* Orestes A. Brownson (1803-1876) was a Vermont-born writer and reformer.
He became a Catholic in 1844. John Hughes (1797-1864), born in Ireland, was
spiritual leader of Catholics in New York from 1837 to his death. He clashed
with Brownson on several issues in the 1850s. [Editor's note]

cism acquired a new aggressive characteristic. Even though the more dom-inant immigrant groups were of a lower strain culturally, their staunch defense of their religion created in this country the most militant Catholic organization in the English speaking world. Before this change the Anglo-American Catholics, like their English brethren, did not show themselves active apologists of the Catholic position, and in striving to advance the Faith by Catholic preeminence in cultural matters they had continued the defeatist attitude of the English minority group of colonial days. The Irish and German Catholic leaders, who were unaccustomed to make any compromises in their relations with non-Catholics, insisted instead on their full rights in all public matters. The position of Bishop Francis Patrick Kenrick in Philadelphia and of Bishop John Hughes in New York on the public schools and on the use of the Catholic Bible in those schools may be open to question on the grounds of strategy but the uncompromising defence of their flocks by these bishops was in the best Catholic tradition. Since that time American Catholicism has never re-treated to the position of a defeatist minority. Nevertheless, since the op-position to the immigrants was based on more than religious disagree-ments there were bound to be some differences within the ranks of the Catholic reaction to the nativistic movement.

Bishops Hughes and Kenrick were not native Americans and repre-sented the immigrant point of view in the public discussions, and the circumstances of the times would not allow any public manifestations of a different point of view by the native-born bishops. Yet there has always been some nativism among the American Catholics. Their patri-otism could have no other results, although Hughes and other episcopal defenders of the immigrants failed to understand that even a Catholic could resent the immigrant invasion. Brownson, as he showed in his *Review,* felt strongly this Yankee resentment towards the immigrant and, in Louisiana, Abbé Adrien Rouquette expressed in French poetry an Americanism that opposed the Irish immigrants and led him to associate with the American Party. And there were other manifestations of this internal cultural conflict in the Catholic group.

Perhaps the locality in which to observe most clearly the amalgamation of these cultural strains into an American Catholic culture was the Middle Western frontier. There the immigrant groups living away from the cities yielded more quickly to the general cultural trends. At least the Catholics in these western settlements—if we except the German mass colonies which were comparable to the Irish groups in the cities—were quickly Americanized. It was noted by the early missionaries in the Middle West that there was less bigotry on the frontier so long as the common problem of conquering the wilderness and the prairies gave little occasion for internecine cultural differences. Generally, the bigotry that appeared on the frontier was an importation from the older settlements, deliberately propagated by missionary societies.

The Americanization of the immigrant Catholic away from the concentrations on the seaboard is shown best in the Kentucky Catholic group which was augmented by Catholics of other nationalities as it spread across the Ohio and Mississippi to found new centers of setltement. These frontiersmen were joined by Irish canal and railroad workers and by German farmers. These English Catholic families—many dating back their arrival to 1681 in Maryland—built up first the communities of Bardstown, Loretto, Holy Cross and the like with Catholic colleges and a seminary, three communities of religious women and a Dominican monastery. Many of these families, such as the Spaldings, Wathens, Coomes, Haydens, Clements and Mattinglys, remained in Kentucky, some at Bardstown and others in more prosperous communities. The same families are also found in Daviess County, Indiana, and in early Catholic communities at Paris, Illinois, and Lancaster, Ohio, and in Tennessee and Missouri. They have given to the Church many bishops and priests and prominent lawyers and physicians. Sometimes when they moved into less Catholic communities they achieved positions of local importance, although the propaganda of the anti-Catholic movements of the forties and fifties usually prevented this. In most communities where Catholics lived, the church or mission chapel with a pastor of almost any national origin was the center of a growing Catholic culture. Usually the Anglo-American element furnished the social leadership of the group and frequently a professional vocation; to this the Irish added spirit and religious fervor and the Germans a devotion to the parish organization and to the parochial school. Seldom were the Catholics the wealthy persons of the community and only the few English or Yankee Catholics were welcomed socially by their non-Catholic neighbors, who wondered at their devotion to Catholic dogma and the Sunday Mass. Only in the completely German communities and in the compact Irish settlements of the eastern cities was the English element lacking, with a resultant cultural isolation that delayed the Americanization of the group.

In the nativist Catholic group there has always been an important small, but vigorous, number of converts and their children. In estimating how many converts there were to the Church among the native Americans during the first two quarters of the century there are no statistics, but some estimates are quite high. These converts were frequently of a higher social position and were less inclined to apologize for their religious differences with the majority. They became far more active than the native Catholics in the propagation and defense of their religion. Notable, besides Eccleston, in the hierarchy, Bishop Josue M. Young of Erie and Bishop James F. Wood of Philadelphia, were converts and there were other notable clerical and lay converts active in the religious discussions of the day. Perhaps none of these outshone in their zeal Isaac Thomas Hecker and Orestes A. Brownson, both of whom became notable for the efforts to show that Catholicism and Americanism were not only compatible but complementary.

In Brownson, particularly, the nativistic attacks on the Irish produced two distinct reactions. Examining the religious attacks on the immigrant, Brownson charged that such attacks were un-American. But to the cultural attack upon the Irish immigrant Brownson was in a certain sense sympathetic, not, as he vehemently insisted, because he was anti-Irish but because he felt that the Irish could best prosper if they joined themselves to the American cultural majority in culture and public practice. Brownson saw only prosperity and advancement for the Irish if they would combine their religious zeal and the advantages of American civilization. But to the Irish American press and to Archbishop John Hughes, for whom Catholicism in the English speaking world and Irish origins had become almost synonymous, writings of this nature from the pen of Brownson amounted to a betrayal of the Faith. The Catholic press attacked Brownson and Archbishop Kenrick allowed his letter of approval of the *Brownson's Review* to be withdrawn. Archbishop Hughes publicly rebuked Brownson at a commencement at Fordham in 1856, to the glee of Thomas D'Arcy McGee's *American Celt*. Disclaiming publicly any intention to injure Brownson, Hughes nevertheless wrote privately to Brownson, ordering him to cease his efforts to make Americanism and Catholicism compatible. Brownson fought vainly against the tide and eventually, after making other tactical errors, had to suspend his *Review* in 1864. Likewise, the concentration of the minds of the American people on the issue of slavery and the approaching Civil War caused a slackening of the interest in the nativistic movement until some years after the war.

Irish immigration never again reached the peak it had attained in the fifties. The Irish who had moved away from the ports of entry and the industrial concentrations tended to assimilate themselves to the more native groups in which they lived, although the compact communities in the eastern cities were more resistant to American culture. The Germans, who generally had sufficient means to buy farmlands, tended to settle in rural communities in the Middle West. As their numbers increased some also settled in Cincinnati, Milwaukee, Chicago, and St. Louis. Only later, as their cultural isolation began to break down, did they feel the effects of this cultural amalgamation and offer resistance to the Americanizing process, paricularly in the so-called Cahensly movement.

During the Civil War the Catholics followed the communities in which they lived to fight for the North or the South. The War lifted for a while the nativistic pressure against the immigrant. Outside of the German communities the leadership was divided between the Irish and their descendants and the old Maryland-Kentucky group, with the latter supplying most of the cultural leaven. Public changes symbolized this fact. During the Civil War Archbishop Hughes was succeeded by the American-born John McCloskey, the first American cardinal, and Archbishop Francis Kenrick was succeeded by the Kentucky-born Martin John Spalding. At the close of the conflict the two groups of native-born and second generation Irish immigrants, together with the other groups not living in compact immigrant groups, had united to form a distinctive American Catholic cultural group. With renewed Irish immigration after the War, American Catholics remained dominantly Irish in numbers and in public policy but the Catholic culture of the whole group became increasingly American. Later conflicts were to arise; first, between the dominantly Irish hierarchy and the foreign language groups, and then between these Americanized groups on the one side and the Irish of the cities and the foreign language groups of the northwest on the other. But throughout these later decades the Americanized Catholic culre remained basically the same as that of 1860 with later immigrants balanced in number by new generations of American-born.

•   •   •

There were some definite advantages and disadvantages in this composite American Catholic culture that was created before 1860. If the Anglo-American group, led by Maréchal, Whitefield and Eccleston and later by Spalding, Bayley and Elder and signalized by activities of such converts as Hecker and Brownson, had retained the dominance over the Catholic minority, perhaps Catholic colleges and an American Catholic literature in English might have flourished more readily. Instead, the energies of this smaller American group that might have developed into higher cultural forms were absorbed in educating and absorbing a larger group which was without means and, in great numbers, had been deprived of education for generations. Likewise, Catholics in politics might even have advanced more quickly in public office if they could have escaped the stigma of foreign culture which the confusion of religion and politics of the nativistic period ascribed to all Catholics. On the credit side, the aggressive American Catholicism which manifests itself in public demonstrations, the frequentation of the sacraments, and the insistence on Catholic parochial schools can be attributed to the tradition of the non-English immigrants, Irish, German, Polish, and the like, who came from Catholic regions of Europe and who saw more quickly the dangers to religious faith in the non-religious public schools and the advantages of a Catholic milieu.

Both natives and immigrants benefited from the freedom of frontier America but the native who was able to remain away from the industrialized urban conditions acquired more quickly a distinctly American spirit. The fact that Catholics who congregated in compact Irish or German settlements in the mill towns, in the larger cities, or even in the immigrant colonization projects of the west made slower progress in accepting American cultural ideals can be explained chiefly by the absence in their communities of members of the Anglo-American Catholic group which had formed the leaven of the Maryland and Kentucky communities. Brownson's analysis of this fact was received angrily in the 1850's. But even then, there were some who sensed the formation of a distinctly American Catholic culture. The writer "M" in the January 1857 *Metropolitan,* the chief Catholic magazine of the time, commenting critically on Brownson's essays on nativism, sized up the situation quite well despite his sympathy for the immigrant group. "The native Catholics of Maryland and Kentucky furnish their full quota of priests and religious, and before there is an increase in the number of native priests there must be an increase in the number of native Catholics. As a general thing Irish priests *ceteris paribus,* are the best for the Irish people and it will be found most likely that the relative number of native priests and native Catholics will under God's providence, augment in proper ratio."

Like so many of the Irish Catholic of the period, "M" did not fully understand that Brownson and Bishops Timon and McGill and Whelan had no doubt of the faith or of the patriotism of the immigrant Catholic. But these native Americans did recognize that there was a distinction between American culture and that of the immigrant. They were convinced that the immigrant could profit by the social and cultural spirit of Americans. The attitude of the Irish immigrant of the fifties was best personified by Archbishop John Hughes. Archbishop Hughes did not seem to understand fully that there had always been American Catholics or that there was no conflict between being an Anglo-American and being a Catholic. Faced with American nativists who were hostile to their religion, the Catholic immigrants can be excused for not realizing that to prefer the ideals of the Anglo-American Catholics was perhaps a greater loyalty to Catholicism and certainly a better service to American Catholic culture. Repelled by the nativists, the immigrants who dominated numerically the Catholic group held back from the common culture and suffered some of the cultural evils which Brownson had predicted as a result of this partial isolation. For the eighty years since 1860 American Catholic culture has risen just as quickly as the immigrant group has been able to Americanize its cultural tradition. Similarly the non-Catholic religious people have shown a better understanding of Catholic culture just in proportion as they have been able to see that the foreign elements of the Catholic culture are the accidents of history and not part of their universal Faith. Those who reject that Faith have other reasons for rejecting American Catholic culture. But the gradual Americanization of the masses of non-English Catholic immigrants, with the old Anglo-American Catholic group as a nucleus, is an understandable process and one as American as all the other combinations of immigration and the frontier which constitute our American civilization.

The Distinctive Tradition of American Catholicism

JAMES HENNESEY, S.J.

While McAvoy analyzed the effects of the American situation on the development of Catholic culture in the United States, a younger scholar, James Hennesey, S.J., of Fordham University, has probed the American influence on official church policy and thinking. The most obvious example of this sort of influence is the American Catholic attitude toward the separation of church and state. Convinced by their own experience of the desirability of separation and religious freedom, American Catholics developed an outlook on these matters that was distinctive in the Catholic world. An American priest, the late John Courtney Murray, S.J., almost single-handedly reformulated Catholic theology on church and state; and the American bishops at the Second Vatican Council were the principal promoters of the Declaration on Religious Freedom adopted by the Council in 1965. Father Hennesey's major work, *The First Council of the Vatican: The American Experience* (1963), shows that the American bishops at the Council of 1869-1870 were as distinctively influenced by their national background as their episcopal successors were at the Second Vatican Council a century later. In the essay reprinted below, Hennesey sketches several dimensions of official Catholic thinking that were shaped by the American social and political environment.

T HE UNDERLYING THESIS OF THIS PAPER IS A SIMPLE ONE: THAT the Roman Catholic Church in the United States developed in a political and social climate radically different from the European, and that its unique development affected its theological thinking in ways

James Hennesey, S.J., "Papacy and Episcopacy in Eighteenth and Nineteenth Century American Catholic Thought," *Records of the American Catholic Historical Society,* LXXVII (September, 1966), 175-189. Reprinted without footnotes by permission of author and the publisher.

that can scarcely be understood if we attempt to fit them into categories conditioned by the European experience. The scope of the paper is a limited one. It deals with one relationship; that of pope and bishops. It makes no effort to treat two obviously co-relative problems, the relationship of bishops to priests and laity. Both problems demand their own full-scale scholarly study.

The paper also rests on an assumption. It is that there has in fact been some theological thought, or at least the raw material for theological thought, in the history of the American church. The assumption has been both ignored and denied. American Catholicism has proved interesting as a sociological phenomenon, as the caretaker of the immigrants, as a force for or against—depending on your point of view—democracy and Americanization, as a perpetrator of anti-intellectualism, and so on. Schools of American church historians have devoted themselves to cataloguing the accomplishments of Catholic heroes, with a heavy emphasis on the hierarchy. For contemporary reasons, some small effort has been made at elucidating an American factual tradition in the matter of church-state relations. But one area about which little has been written, presumably because there was little to write, is that of the contribution of the church in the United States to the development of theological thought. It is in this deficiency that the most startling contrast exists between the historiography of American Catholicism and American Protestantism. We know a great deal about what American Catholic churchmen *did;* we know comparatively much less about what they *said* and *thought.* An essay on the development of a collegial notion of the hierarchy is but a small contribution to the overall picture. But it does suggest that there are still huge, untapped resources available to the researcher.

The recent and decisive influence of the American tradition in the formulation of Vatican II's Declaration on Religious Freedom suggests that the negative consensus about theological thought in the American church may be in error, and that a church that developed within a revolutionary and constitutional structure and in religio-social surroundings vastly different from the European model may have other contributions to make. In the area of papal-episcopal relations, an examination of the several stages of the church's development in this country is instructive. The story is a paradoxical one. The paradox is suggested in the following quotations.

The first is taken from a letter addressed to the bishops of the United States on April 15, 1902 by Pope Leo XIII:

> Your chief praise is that you have promoted and sedulously continue to foster the union of your churches with this chief of churches and with the Vicar of Christ on earth.

The second quotation comes from the Pastoral Letter of the bishops assembled at the Third Provincial Council of Baltimore, held in 1837. The bishops first protested that they "acknowledged the spiritual and ecclesiastical supremacy of the chief bishop of our church, the pope or bishop of Rome," but then they added:

> We do not acknowledge any civil or political supremacy, or power over us, in any foreign potentate or power, though that potentate might be the chief pastor of our church.

The curious thing about those bishops of a century or so ago was that they were substantially as ultramontane* as a Manning in England or a Cullen in Ireland, but at the same time they maintained an independent stance and they were clear that their loyalty was a loyalty in spiritual matters and not in politics. The European mind found this difficult, if not impossible, to understand. After a conversation in 1853 with Orestes Brownson, the young Sir John Acton came away with the impression, as he wrote to Ignaz Döllinger, that "all the American theologians were thorough ultramontanes, partisans of the personal infallibility of the pope." It was not that simple. Sixteen years later, in the fall of 1869, Richard Simpson, Acton's collaborator in promoting the liberal Catholic cause in Britain, expressed his puzzlement in a letter to Acton, who was then living in Rome. Simpson had just met several of the North American bishops on their way to the first session of the First Vatican Council. He reported to Acton, who was interested in securing recruits for the anti-infallibilist cause:

> I think that the English and Irish bishops should be acted upon through the Americans, who are perfectly misunderstood at Rome. They have the art of hiding an uncompromising resistance under the show of the most hearty loyalty and so they are more listened to than we are, who, if we resist, generally resist without that show.

* "Ultramontane" was the term applied to those who favored increasing the power and authority of the pope in the mid-nineteenth century. [Editor's note]

The uniquely American attitude towards the papacy in the eighteenth and nineteenth centuries is brought out in the combination of these statements. The church in the United States has been loyal to the Pope. But it understood its loyalty in a way in which the European, accustomed to the extremes of union or of violent separation of altar and throne never could. Simpson had to conclude that the Americans were Machiavellian. They were not. They simply did not think in age old European categories.

THE COLONIAL PERIOD

The Roman Catholic Church in English America was established in 1634. For the next century and a half, it was administered almost entirely by Jesuit missionaries operating within the structure of their religious order and following the direction of their own superiors. For the first 150 years of its American development, the distinctively 'episcopal' Roman Catholic Church had a definitely 'presbyterian' cast to it, and these presbyterian origins of church government left their mark on the initial stages of Catholic development in the territory of the United States.

The reasons for the anomalous situation of the church in colonial America are not difficult to find. England was a long way away. The Roman Catholic Church in the mother country was itself reorganized along episcopal lines only in 1685, with the appointment of the first of a succession of vicars-apostolic. Father Henry Harrison, who had taught at the Jesuit school in downtown New York from 1684 to 1689, wrote in 1695 that "all the missionaries depended solely on their regular superiors." The first clear exercise of episcopal jurisdiction dated from 1721 and not until 1757 did Rome formally grant ecclesiastical jurisdiction in the colonies to the London vicar-apostolic, who then continued to exercise it, in a very distant way, until the American Revolution.

The lack of juridical clarity and the physical separation of the colonies from England meant that the Church developed in relative autonomy. Two of the church's seven sacraments, holy orders and confirmation, were never administered. This was one of the matters which bothered Bishop Challoner of London, and led him to suggest that a bishop or vicar-apostolic be appointed. The reaction from America to this suggestion was consistently negative almost up to the eve of Bishop John Carroll's appointment in

1789. There were several reasons for this, some of them rooted in Europe's conflicts, others stemming from the delicate situation of Catholics in England's colonies.

Apart from a small band of Franciscans who were in Maryland from 1672 to 1720, the American missionaries were all English Jesuits. The story of conflict between the secular clergy and the Jesuits and other regulars in England from the time of Elizabeth I is not a particularly happy one. The prolonged secular-regular controversy which scarred English Catholic history for the whole period of the colonies' existence inevitably influenced the Maryland Jesuits in the direction of autonomy from episcopal control. But as time went on, they also began to have problems with the Roman Congregation of the Propagation of the Faith, founded in 1622 by Pope Gregory XV. Problems with Progaganda were not limited to America. There were difficulties over the question of the Chinese Rites and in England and Scotland and elsewhere. Whatever the truth or the right in these controversies, the fact remains that they helped the Jesuits in Maryland and Pennsylvania to develop attitudes hostile to the Roman Congregation, and these attitudes were sharpened by the suppression of the Jesuit order by Pope Clement XIV in 1773.

The difficulties of setting up a more normal form of church government in the colonies were compounded by the local situation. Religious toleration was not one of the ornaments of colonial America. The Catholic laity of Maryland were well aware of their parlous state, and on July 16, 1765 a group of 265 laymen addressed to the Jesuit Provincial in England the following memorandum on the subject of the appointment of a vicar-apostolic:

> Hon. Sir. Having received intelligence that a plan is on foot for sending into this province an Apostolic Vicar, we think it our duty to God, ourselves and posterity, to represent our objections to such a measure; as what would give our adversaries, bent on our ruin, a stronger handle than anything they have hitherto been able to lay hold on, and consequently terminate in the utter extirpation of our holy religion. . . .

The petitioners, headed by Charles Carroll II, reminded the Provincial that the presence of a bishop would not only furnish a new pretext for persecution, but that it would transgress the legal limitations under which they lived. And they argued also that the official Anglican Church had not as yet been able to establish a bishopric in America. On the same day, Charles Carroll addressed a letter repeating the same arguments to Bishop Challoner, in which he assured the Vicar-Apostolic of London that he wrote "in order to continue in the enjoyment of my spiritual peace, and a quiet possession of my temporal goods, and from these motives only," and not "at the instigation of the Jesuits.

In answer to the suggestion in 1771 that the Bishop of Quebec come south to administer confirmation, Father Ferdinand Farmer, missionary in Philadelphia, wrote that the coming of a bishop would "create great disturbances, with the danger of depriving us of the paltry privileges which we are now enjoying, especially in Maryland, where the exercise, even in private, of our Religion rests upon no authority." He went on to say that it was "incredible how hateful to non-Catholics in all parts of America is the very name of Bishop, even to such as should be members of the Church which is called Anglican." Farmer also remarked that sentiment in the colonies was strongly against the concession that the British government had made in allowing continuance of the bishopric of Quebec. In consequence of this letter, the project was cancelled. That Farmer's fears were not groundless is obvious to anyone who has read the 1774 Suffolk Resolves or the Address of the Continental Congress to the People of Great Britain. There was a genuine fear abroad in the land that a "religion fraught with sanguinary and impious tenets" might be introduced south of the border and "reduce the ancient free Protestant colonies to the same state of slavery with themselves." Hardly the appropriate atmosphere for the introduction of a Papist bishop!

Execution of the suppression of the Society of Jesus in English America was committed to Bishop Challoner, who in 1773 sent the following report to Rome on the American church:

> All that we have learned from the relation of others about the state of religion in those parts is that in the provinces of Maryland and Pennsylvania of North America there are many thousands of Catholics, under about 16 Jesuit missionaries, who set a good example to their flock, but do not want a bishop at all.

These words serve as Challoner's valedictory to the American Church. Although theoretically the American missions continued under his jurisdiction until his death in 1781 and then came under his successor, Bishop James Talbot, the English jurisdiction in fact ceased with the outbreak of the American Revolution. This was recognized on both sides of the

Atlantic and was acknowledged formally by Talbot in 1783, when he declined to grant ecclesiastical faculties to two American priests who were returning to their homeland.

The picture that emerges from the colonial period is that of a segment of the church operating more or less independently of episcopal control, and in considerable isolation from Rome. The feeling of isolation was heightened by the break in communications occasioned by the Revolution and also by the missionaries' sense of loss at the suppression of the religious order to which they had belonged.* At the same time, the isolation was a blessing in that it enabled the church in the United States to develop its own personality within and along with the new nation. Disestablishment of the various Protestant churches and the proclamation of religious libery in the new republic were welcomed by the Catholics. John Carroll wrote exultantly to his English correspondent Charles Plowden that "in these United States our religious system has undergone a revolution, if possible, more extraordinary than our political one." The spirit of nationalism engendered by the Revolution carried over into ecclesiastical matters also.

FEDERAL PERIOD

During the Revolution, administration of the church in the United States was, practically speaking, dormant. A change came with the emergence of John Carroll, an ex-Jesuit, cousin of Charles Carroll of Carrollton and brother of Daniel Carroll, signer of both the Articles of Confederation and the Constitution. In 1782 Carroll drew up a proposal which provided the basis of future church organization in the United States. The principal focus of Carroll's plan was the temporal administration of the estates belonging to the ex-Jesuits, but he had other purposes also: "to perpetuate a succession of labourers in the vineyard, to preserve their morals, to prevent idleness, and to secure an equitable and frugal administration of our temporals." In the plan occurred a section which reflected the ex-Jesuit distrust of the Roman Curia, when Carroll pointed out:

---

* The Jesuit order was suppressed everywhere except in Russia by papal order in 1773. It was fully reconstituted by a later pope in 1814. [Editor's note]

that the English ex-Jesuits had rightly distinguished between the spiritual power derived from the Bishop, and which must be left in the hands to which he had intrusted it; and the common rights of the missioners to their temporal possessions, to which, as the Bishop, or Pope himself, have no just claim, so neither can they invest any person or persons with the administration of them.

This theme, distinguishing papal and episcopal spiritual authority from temporal authority, appeared regularly in Carroll's correspondence. On September 26, 1783, he wrote

A foreign temporal jurisdiction will never be tolerated here; and even the spiritual supremacy of the Pope is the only reason why in some of the United States the full participation of all civil rights is not granted to Roman Catholics.

On April 10, 1784, Carroll returned to the same theme when he wrote:

But this you may be assured of, that no authority derived from the Propaganda will ever be admitted here; that the Catholic Clergy and Laity here know that the only connection they ought to have with Rome is to acknowledge the Pope as Spiritual head of the Church; that no Congregation existing in his States shall be allowed to exercise any share of his Spiritual authority here; that no Bishop Vicar Apostolical shall be admitted, and, if we are to have a Bishop, he shall not be *in partibus* (a refined Roman political contrivance), but an ordinary national Bishop, in whose appointment Rome shall have no share, so that we are very easy about their machinations. Our Brethren here, in a meeting held last October, settled or nearly settled a plan of internal government, which will meet with your approbation, being founded on Christian and rational principles.

Carroll's nationalistic sentiments come through very clearly. The question of the extent of the pope's spiritual jurisdiction was one that preoccupied him, and in which he seems to have been influenced by the English priest Joseph Berington, who in 1788 advised him:

Certainly were I circumstanced as you in America seem to be I would shut my eyes on the 14 last centuries, and only consider what was the prerogative of the See of Rome during the Apostolic ages and the years immediately succeeding to them. All that is *essential* then existed; the rest is abuse and usurpation.

It was in the course of his correspondence with Berington that Carroll approached the question of a national church from another angle when he said that a vernacular liturgy was "essential to the service of God and the benefit of mankind," and declared that "to continue the practice of the Latin liturgy in the present state of things must be owing either to chimerical fears of innovation or to indolence and inattention in the first pastors of the national churches in not joining to solicit or indeed ordain this necessary alteration."

On June 9, 1784, John Carroll was appointed by Rome as Ecclesiastical Superior of the "Mission in the thirteen United States of North America." He was also informed of the pope's intention to follow this by appointment of a vicar-apostolic. These arrangements were not to Carroll's liking, and in July, 1785, a letter came from Rome announcing that the project of a vicar-apostolic was suspended, and that when the time came for a bishop, the missionaries themselves might propose two or three names for the post. Carroll's real opposition was not to the appointment of a bishop, but to the appointment of a vicar-apostolic whose tenure would be at the pleasure of Roman authorities. He wrote:

> You well know that in our free and jealous government, where Catholics are admitted into all public councils equally with the professors of any other religion, it will never be suffered that their ecclesiastical Superior (be he Bishop or Prefect-Apostolic) receive his appointment from a foreign State, and only hold it at the discretion of a foreign tribunal or congregation.

There was one more curious episode in this matter of the choice of the first bishop. Rome was used to dealing with civil governments in the question of episcopal nominations. In 1783, Benjamin Franklin and the Papal Nuncio in Paris entered into discussions about providing a bishop for the United States. Franklin inquired of Congress, and received in return the statement Congress had no competence in the matter. A new era in church-state relations was beginning.

The clergy of the United States had a voice in the selection of the first three bishops appointed. The General Chapter of the Clergy, meeting at Whitemarsh, Maryland, presented the name of John Carroll to Rome, and he was named first Bishop of Baltimore in 1789. He traveled to England for his consecration in company with James Madison, who was to be consecrated first Episcopalian Bishop of Virginia. Two coadjutor bishops, Lawrence Graessl and Leonard Neale, were subsequently elected by the

General Chapter. Carroll and some of his senior priests also had a voice in the choice of the first suffragan bishops of the metropolitan see of Baltimore. After that the pendulum swung and Roman nominations came into style, but not without considerable complaint on this side of the ocean, especially when there was question of naming foreign priests to American dioceses.

NATIONAL PERIOD

The organizational years of the church in the United States coincided with the tremendous upheaval of the French Revolutionary era in Europe. Understandably, the popes and the Roman Curia were more concerned with the Revolution and with Napoleon than they were with the little group of Catholics in faraway America. In addition, Pope Pius VI was Napoleon's captive from 1798-1799 and his successor, Pius VII, was an imperial prisoner for five years, from 1809 to 1814. The church in the English colonies had developed in isolation from the mainstream of Catholic life; the church in the United States did the same. The period of relative isolation from the central government of the Church therefore really lasted very nearly 200 years.

The early part of the 19th century was a turbulent time for the Catholic Church in America. There were problems with lay trustees, with recalcitrant priests, and with foreign meddlers in American ecclesiastical affairs. The net result was to force a strong episcopal posture. Cut off to a large extent from Rome, the bishops developed in an independent way. Within the hierarchy, conflict developed between bishops of Irish and of French lineage. There are two schools of thought here. One holds strongly that the Irish made the better adjustment to American ways: the other is equally strong in maintaining that it was the French who really continued the traditions of the old Maryland Catholics. Whatever the truth, the fact of conflict is certain.

There were other characteristics which developed in those years. With the coming of the immigrants, the bishops became more and more paternalistic. As the old American stock reacted more and more unfavorably to the foreigners, bishops and priests became active apologists. They engaged in strong polemics and they became interested in politics as a weapon. In the face of Nativism, they were conscious of the need to be

"American" and they actively opposed efforts to appoint foreign bishops here. It was in this context that the Third Provincial Council of Baltimore issued the pastoral letters quoted earlier.

CONCILIAR AND COLLEGIAL TRADITION

In the long run, one of the most significant developments in the early part of the 19th century was the growth of a conciliar and collegial tradition in the United States which was unequalled in the western church. Before the establishment of the Diocese of Baltimore in 1789, the clergy of the United States had handled the problems of church government in three General Chapters of the Clergy held at Whitemarsh, Maryland, between 1783 and 1789. Meetings were also held in three districts into which the clergy divided themselves. In 1791, Bishop Carroll held at Baltimore a diocesan synod which continued the collegial tradition and which legislated on matters like education, Matrimony, liturgy and church administration. In 1810, Carroll met in a similar meeting with his newly consecrated suffragan bishops. For a variety of reasons, the tradition was then suspended for 19 years, until 1829, and the First Provincial Council of Baltimore. The calling of the Council represented a victory for John England, the Irish-born Bishop of Charleston, and a man who in his own diocese established a diocesan constitution with representative houses of clergy and laity. Six more Baltimore Provincial Councils met in the next twenty years. In each case, all the bishops of the country were present, and their legislation was binding on the Catholics of the entire nation. These were not merely meetings to discuss problems; they were legislative assemblies. The same, of course, is true of the three Plenary Councils of Baltimore, held in 1852, 1866 and 1884. There is no other national church within the Roman Catholic communion which met so regularly and legislated so widely.

RELATIONS WITH THE PAPACY

The conciliar tradition established at Baltimore could not help but affect the thinking of the American hierarchy. At the same time, the bishops were under continued pressure from the political, intellectual and social climate in which they lived. The same basic problem which had affected John Carroll and the old Maryland Catholics affected them: their church seemed alien in America. And the fact that its constituency was increased each year by thousands and then hundreds of thousands of foreign immigrants strengthened the impression. Throughout, the attitude of the American bishops remained constant. They yielded to none in their devotion to the pope, but their loyalty was a spiritual loyalty, not mixed with political considerations, as it generally was in Europe. In 1838, Francis Patrick Kenrick, Coadjutor Bishop of Philadelphia and the most respectable American Catholic theologian of the period explained:

> . . . secular concerns are not, of themselves, subject to . . . [the pope's] cognizance: and the complicated social relations which arise from the free acts of individuals, or from public law, or from the action of [the] civil authorities, are not the matter of his judgment, unless they involve a violation of the great principles of Christian morality.

The American bishops carried this theory into practice on several occasions. They opposed the semi-official visit in 1853 of Archbishop Gaetano Bedini, who was sent by Rome to investigate American church matters and the possibility of a Papal Nuncio here. The 1864 Syllabus of Errors was received politely, but hardly enthusiastically, and in private the bishops expressed their concern. Archbishop John McCloskey of New York wrote to Archbishop [Martin J.] Spalding of Baltimore:

> It is consoling to think and believe that our Holy Father has in all his official acts a light and guidance from on High—for according to all the rules of mere human prudence and wisdom the encyclical with its annex of condemned propositions would be considered ill timed.

Other instances of independent American judgment of Roman decisions were to occur in the 1860's, when the bishops forcefully rejected in a published statement any notion of enlisting an American volunteer force for the defense of the Papal States, as was being done elsewhere in the world. This was not to say that they did not sympathize with Pius IX and his troubles, but they wanted nothing to do with armed intervention in his struggle with Italy, nor did they consider retention of the Papal States essential to the Papacy, as many European theologians did.

Once again on a theoretical level, American bishops showed the influence of their tradition at the time of the definition of the dogma of the Immaculate Conception in 1854. Archbishop Kenrick of Balimore and Bishop O'Connor of Pittsburgh were among those who attended a meeting in Rome preliminary to the promulgation of the dogma. The meeting's competence had been restricted by the Roman authorities to matters of style, but the two Americans were prominent among those whose objections resulted in an entire re-drafting of the document. Both pointed to misuse of evidence from Scripture, the Fathers and conciliar tradition, while O'Connor asked that it be made clear that the definition was being made "with the consent of the bishops." In this he echoed the thought of Archbishop Kenrick, who in 1839 had written an explanation of the existence of the episcopal college, both when the bishops were gathered in council and when they were dispersed in their sees. Kenrick had also argued that infallible papal decrees demanded at least the tacit consent of the *collegium episcopale.*

The notion of collective episcopal authority in the church was reiterated in the decrees of the Second Plenary Council of Baltimore in 1866. The bishops at that time placed themselves on record as upholding the prerogatives and place of the pope in the church, but they went on to balance that statement with a paragraph on the role of the college of bishops:

> Bishops, therefore, who are the successors of the Apostles, and whom the Holy Spirit has placed to rule the Church of God, which He acquired with His own blood, agreeing and judging together with its head on earth, the Roman Pontiff, whether they are gathered in general councils, or dispersed throughout the world, are inspired from on high with the gift of inerrancy, so that their body or college can never fail in faith nor define anything against any doctrine revealed by God.

This same theme was resumed in the Pastoral Letter of 1866, where the bishops argued that Christ gave "to the Apostles, as a Ministerial Body which was to have perpetual existence by the perpetual succession of its members" the powers He Himself had received from His Father.

THE VATICAN COUNCIL

The majority of the American bishops summoned to the First Vatican Council in 1869 were opposed to defining the dogma of papal infallibility.

We have this on the testimony of Cardinal Gibbons, who was himself a participant in the Council. The testimony is borne out by the facts. Their reasons varied. A catechism widely used in the United States up until Vatican I contained the following question and answer:

> Q. Must not Catholics believe the Pope in himself to be infallible?
> A. This is a Protestant invention; it is no article of Catholic faith; no decision of his can oblige under pain of heresy unless it be received and enforced by the teaching body; that is, by the bishops of the church.

Some bishops had genuine doubts about the historical and theological evidence. One of them, Bernard McQuaid of Rochester, later explained: "Somehow or other it was in my head that the bishops ought to be consulted" in the matter of infallible pronouncements. Archbishop Peter Kenrick of St. Louis, the leading American opponent, reconciled himself to the dogma only, as he wrote Lord Acton, by applying Newman's theory of development to it. Most of the Americans were what came to be called inopportunists. They agreed that the dogma could be defined, but they had strong reservations as to the desirability of doing so. All through the council, from the opening session, they were strong for episcopal rights, whether on procedural matters or in substantials. They demanded that the wording of the Constitution on Faith include a statement to show that in a council the pope and the bishops defined docrine. They took a dim view of the insistence that the word "Roman" be included in the official name of the church. They pointed out that the principle of unity in the church was Christ and not Peter. In the matter of papal primacy of jurisdiction, it was an American, Spalding of Baltimore, who secured inclusion of a statement to the effect that the ordinary jurisdiction [was that] of residential bishops. In these and in all their conciliar activities, the Americans revealed a pronounced pastoral sense. They were also more aware than the vast majority of their colleagues of the existence of Christians outside the Roman communion, and they worked to have the conciliar decrees reflect that awareness. In the end, the Americans had very little influence on the conciliar decrees. All of them accepted them without reservation. The man probably most troubled, the Archbishop of St. Louis, explained that he did so from a motive of obedience to the church and on faith. In the heated climate of the time, with the Italian Army knocking on Rome's gates, explanations were not given, and Vatican I's constitution on the church emphasized the position of the pope without giving balanced treatment to that of the bishops. A century later the balance was righted in the constitution on the church of Vatican II. The Americans of a century ago would have felt more at home in the Rome of the 1960's.

THE END OF THE CENTURY

Thus far I have been speaking about the attitudes of bishops in this question of the relationship of episcopacy and papacy. Emphasis has been on what might be termed the 'political aspect' of the question, that is, the relationship of bishops to Rome in their ordinary and extraordinary dealings with the Holy See. The distance to Rome, the general American tendency to non-involvement in European affairs, the unique American outlook on politico-religious matters, the whole experience of building a church in a pluralistic society in a new world, all of these factors influenced the thinking of leaders of the American church.

There were other forces at work too. Solid devotion to the papacy always co-existed with the independent stance we have been talking about. On a more speculative level this found voice in the writings of Francis X. Weninger, missionary extraordinary in the mid-West in the middle years of the century, whose book on infallibility was as ultramontane as any produced in Europe. There were imported influences also. Even in the 19th century American Catholics read French ecclesiastical writers. In 1829 Bishop Benedict Fenwick of Boston reported that reading Joseph de Maistre's *Du Pape* had completely converted him to belief in papal infallibility. Among laymen, James A. McMaster, longtime editor of the New York Freeman's Journal, was an infallibilist and a papalist in every respect. He was an equally strong gadfly of bishops and advocate of the rights of parish clergy. His general thesis in reporting the First Vatican Council was that the bishops had been summoned to Rome to be taught "a lesson in faith." His targets he described as "the little handful of frivolous men in episcopal position who want to make a fuss." Yet it is worth noting that McMaster welcomed the suspension of United States-Papal diplomatic relations in 1868. He found the concept offensive to Protestants and Catholics alike.

The nineteenth century was one of the great ages of Roman centralization. Doctrinally, it produced the papal definition of the Immaculate Conception and Vatican I's definitions of papal primacy and infallibility. All of these highlighted the central role of the pope. In many lesser ways, the same trend was evident. The American church could scarcely remain untouched by this mainstream trend. In the 1850's Rome had expressed its concern at possible excessive nationalism in the United States when it refused the Archbishop of Baltimore the honorary title of Primate, which had been requested by the bishops. The years following Vatican I saw the Roman hold strengthened. More American graduates of the American College in Rome moved into positions of power, communications improved, travel became more frequent. Internal problems of the church were referred to Rome for solution.

Since John Carroll's time, there had been tensions in the relationship between priests and bishops. There were no canonical parishes in the United States, and bishops therefore had a rather arbitrary control over pastors. The controversy, involving politics, economic theories and ecclesiastical obedience, between Archbishop Corrigan of New York and Father Edward McGlynn was long and painful and very public. The predominantly Irish hierarchy clashed with various national groups. There were controversies over parochial schools, the Catholic University of America, the Knights of Labor. The church in America became sophisticated with the nation and it attracted more and more of Rome's attention. The return to positions of power in Rome of Italians like Cardinal Camillo Mazzella and Father Salvatore Brandi, who had spent time in the United States and even become citizens, is an aspect of the question not yet really explored.

These problems led to the establishment in 1893 of the Apostolic Delegation in Washington. Rome had long been interested in having a papal representative in the United States. The 1853 expedition of Archbishop Gaetano Bedini ended in fiasco. An effort to name an Italian prelate presiding officer of the 1884 Third Plenary Council of Baltimore was blocked by the American bishops. But in 1893 the appointment of Archbishop Francesco Satolli as Apostolic Delegate was a *fait accompli,* even as a letter from Cardinal Gibbons of Baltimore protesting the move was on its way to Rome.

Opposition to the Delegate's appointment was considerable and vocal. Bishop [John Lancaster] Spalding of Peoria declared publicly that the

English-speaking world wanted to manage its own affairs and he spoke darkly of the meaning of the Monroe Doctrine and of the fate of Emperor Maximilian of Mexico. He stated unequivocally: "There is and has been for years, in the Catholic Church of the United States, a deep feeling of opposition to the appointment of a permanent Delegate for this country." In words reminiscent of John Carroll, he continued: "American Catholics are devoted to the church. They recognize in the pope Christ's vicar and gladly receive from him doctrines of faith and morals. But for the rest, they ask him to interfere as little as may be."

There is more in the same vein. But we have come to the final decade of the century. Controversies continued, the role of the Apostolic Delegate increased, and the American church became more and more used to having its problems solved by Roman Congregations. The crises over Americanism and Modernism threw a cloud over the more daring excursions of independent thought. The early years of the twentieth century formed a real watershed in the history of American Catholicism. Vital contact with the past, the past of the Maryland missions, John Carroll, the conciliar and collegial tradition, was largely lost. Many of the ideas which we hear being preached today germinated in the American Catholic church of the past. It is a past worth reconsidering. It is a tradition which should not be lost.

Catholics, Protestants, and Public Education

VINCENT P. LANNIE

The "school question" has been a perennial issue in the adjustment of Catholics to American society. Hardly a decade has gone by since the 1830s without some sort of controversy over Catholicism and education. This is not surprising, considering the crucial place of the public school in the thinking of Americans. The school, after all, is expected to open the doors of individual opportunity, to make good citizens, and to insure a harmonious blending of people of the most diverse backgrounds. It is a key institution in our national life and any serious strain in American society is almost sure to be reflected in the schools. The first major episode in the long controversy over Catholicism and education took place in New York in 1840. Vincent P. Lannie, historian of education at the University of Notre Dame, has recently given us a detailed account of the dispute that arose when Bishop John Hughes tried to get public funds for Catholic schools in his diocese. Hughes failed in this attempt, but his efforts resulted in breaking the hold over New York City schools of a private, non-denominational Protestant group which had previously controlled educational funds. In the conclusion to his study, reproduced below, Lannie evaluates the outcome and implications of this contest, and points out its connection with the subsequent drive to set up a system of Catholic parochial schools and with the secularization of the public schools.

Reprinted by permission from Vincent P. Lannie, *Public Money and Parochial Education: Bishop Hughes, Governor Seward and the New York School Controversy*, pp. 245-258. Cleveland: The Press of Case Western Reserve University, 1968. Copyright © 1968 by The Press of Case Western Reserve University. Footnotes have been omitted.

I

"IN ORDER TO UNDERSTAND THE AMERICAN PEOPLE ONE MUST UNderstand their belief in education." And in order to understand this American commitment to education, it is necessary to understand the integral relationship between education and the political life of the nation. For American education has long been affected by numerous political coalitions that have insisted upon specific educational directions within different historical frameworks.

The New York school question was a case in point, for it was essentially a political issue. Since a political body was competent to grant or deny relief, the political complexion of New York was crucial to any solution of the educational question. No sooner did immigrants step from their dirty and crowded ships than the Democratic party accepted them with open arms. The Whigs, on the other hand, early exhibited a marked antagonism to foreigners as aliens, as Catholics, and as members of a lower social and economic class. George Templeton Strong represented this negative Whig feeling when he characterized immigrants as "Wretched, filthy, bestial-looking Italians and Irish, and creations that looked as if they had risen from the lazarettos of Naples . . . ; in short, the very scum and dregs of human nature. . . . A dirty Irishman is bad enough, but he's nothing comparable to a nasty French or Italian loafer."

Yet it was a Whig governor who precipitated the school dispute by urging state support for Catholic schools. Although he received some upstate Whig support, New York City Whigs never endorsed his measure, and led the vanguard of opposition during the entire dispute. Almost naturally, Seward became closely associated with the Whig-inclined Catholic bishop of New York, and this episcopal-gubernatorial coalition never faltered during the three-year struggle. Instead of condemning outright any school legislation favorable to Catholics, the Democrats at first skirted the issue since they considered Whig opposition strong enough to prevent its passage. The Democratic party had a chance to solidify and perhaps even to increase its Catholic support at the November, 1841, election, but the party preferred to remain ambiguous on the school question. Thereupon, Hughes swung ino political action and organized the "Carroll Hall" ticket while the nativists retaliated with the Union ticket.

Even though the Catholics ran against three opposition parties, they emerged as an important balance of power not only within the Democratic party but also in New York City politics. Since the Democratic party could not afford subsequent Catholic defection, it was forced to sponsor legislation which would remedy, at least in part, Catholic educational complaints. Thus, Democratic assemblymen joined forces with Seward Whigs and supporters of Hughes and easily engineered the Maclay school bill through the Assembly. Tammany Hall then arranged a political deal between Scott and Corning so that the amended school bill was able to squeak through the Senate.* Passage of the school bill quickly returned the Catholic Irish to the Democratic fold, in time for New York City's municipal election. The Whig-nativist alliance elicited the wrath of Seward and partly influenced his decision to withdraw temporarily from public life. But his position on the school question was not forgotten by his enemies. Not only did it cost him Whig support in the early 1840's, but it also played a role in his being denied the Republican presidential nomination two decades later in 1860. Hughes wisely remained aloof from further partisan political involvements though he could never live down his reputation as a political manipulator. In his reminiscences, which he wrote toward the end of his life, he still smarted because all his efforts to blunt this reputation had failed—even though he concluded unconvincingly that "I have long since ceased to trouble myself about this erroneous impression." It is clear that, in successive stages, it was an upstate Whig-Roman Catholic-Democratic coalition that passed the New York school bill in 1842. Nativist pressure and city Whig political power were insufficient to block the coalition even though the Catholics never achieved their primary goal. Only because the Catholic claim was endorsed by the majority political fusion—whether out of conviction or from political expediency—did Catholics receive

* Before the passage of the Maclay school law in April, 1842, control of educational funds in the city of New York was in the hands of the Public School Society, a non-sectarian but definitely Protestant association. The Maclay bill met Catholic grievances in that it displaced this private society, objectionable to Catholics on religious grounds, and vested control of educational funds in the hands of an elected school board in each ward of the city. Catholic schools were still ineligible for funds, however, because the law forbade giving any public money to a school in which sectarian religious doctrines were taught. [Editor's note]

even "partial redress." But neither side achieved a complete victory in the controversy—a result not uncommon in the delicate interplay of educational and political forces in American society.

II

And so the school question had come to a close. Or had it? Hughes remained convinced of the justice in the Catholic position. New York City's public schools were religiously unacceptable to Catholics, and therefore he sought public subsidization of Catholic schools. To this end he used all his powers of persuasion. He represented a united Catholic front; he petitioned the Common Council for relief; and he debated his opponents before this municipal body. After the first Catholic legislative ventures met with a temporizing postponement, Hughes played a bold hand and organized an independent political ticket to emphasize Catholic unanimity and determination. But when the State Legislature finally passed the amended Maclay bill in 1842, Catholics were really no better off than they had been in 1840. Hughes had sought public funds for Catholic schools, and he received instead public schools allegedly devoid of sectarianism.

True, the Public School Society's monopoly had been broken, and astute observers began to count the death knell of this once powerful organization. It was now obvious that the Society's days were numbered. With "melancholy forebodings of the future," the trustees issued their thirty-seventh Annual Report in May, 1842. They reiterated their belief that the new school legislation would subject public education to the blighting influence of partisan politics and sectarian animosity. The educational superiority of the Society's schools was "overthrown" and the "glory of their system . . . dimmed, they fear, forever." The report acknowledged that the death blow had been struck and that it was just a matter of time before the Society closed its doors. Nevertheless, the trustees would continue their work until the new and "impractical" system finally "impaired" and "destroyed" the educational glory that was New York. Eleven years of parallel existence with New York City's district school system under the Board of Education had convinced both groups that such an overlapping situation was not feasible. And so in

1853, after forty-eight years of educational service, the Public School Society delivered its final dirge, surrendered its independent trust to city authorities, and turned its schools over to the district school system, where they became an indistinguishable part of the educational system of New York City. In this connection, contemporary accounts bitterly acknowledged the "triumph of the Roman Catholics."

But if Hughes had succeeded, it was a pyrrhic victory. His episcopal colleague in Philadelphia, Francis Kenrick, thought that Hughes had been "fairly worsted" in the school dispute. When the Common Council had initially denied the Catholic application for school funds, Bishop John England of Charleston wrote that he quite expected such a decision. Catholics could expect this unfair treatment to continue because of the mounting prejudice against them among their fellow Americans:

> We write deliberately when we state that, probably, there is not a town or city council in the United States that would not have decided in the same way. . . . We do not think it likely that a public body can be found in the United States which does not, without its own consciousness or suspicion, think and act under the influence of great prejudice against Catholics, their claims, their rights, their principles, their religion, and their politics. . . . It is, therefore, that we said that the Catholic cannot expect justice from any public body in this country, because every such body is more or less under the influence of that prejudice which we have so imperfectly described.

Although Hughes realized that the new school law did not grant the "positive benefit" which Catholics had sought, he thought that it provided "the triumph of a principle" and vindicated both Seward's and his efforts. In a letter to Seward, he expressed deep gratitude for the governor's efforts in achieving a measure of educational justice for New York Catholics. "With all its imperfections," Hughes believed that the act would "be of considerable service to the diffusion of knowledge in this city among that class who stand most in need of it, and who have been hitherto most neglected." When he penned his reminiscences in 1858, he continued this line of reasoning. He characterized the new law as a "partial redress" and still gloried that it doomed the Public School Society's "wicked monopoly which claimed to take charge of the minds and hearts of Catholic children." Even though the district school system was "very different indeed, from what I would have recommended," nevertheless Hughes described it as "an immense improvement on the one which it replaced."

Years after the dispute, there was still confusion in the public mind, both Catholic and non-Catholic, concerning its outcome. When the Catholics of New Orleans were preparing in 1851 to seek public funds for their schools, Archbishop Anthony Blanc communicated with Hughes for clarification as to the success of New York Catholics in their quest for public aid:

> I am anxious to know from yourself, how far you succeeded in the attempt you made in New York some years ago. Some have been under the impression that you obtained such a proportion of funds as you desired; others say you were not altogether unsuccessful, though you did not obtain all you desired, without being able to say exactly what was the nature of the benefit you derived from the contest.

In his reply, Hughes summarized the issues and encouraged Blanc to make the fight for public support even though the request would no doubt be rejected:

> *Our* school contest has resulted in a very great amelioration. Before it began the whole common school education in the city was in the hands of a close corporation composed of bigots. Now it is open, and Catholics have the power to be and to appoint their own school commissioners, according to their numbers in different wards in the city, but still under general laws which I think unjust and inexpedient. I took good care never to express myself satisfied with the change, altho' it was much for the better. We, as Catholics, have not, nor do I desire that we should have, any right or authority to expend public money in support of public education, at least when all will be convinced that for the benefit of the country, a change is desirable.
>
> I will say to you, that my great object was to establish this question on the right basis, in however small a district. I did not succeed, but at least I did something in the right direction towards success. Time, I trust will do the rest. . . .
>
> Fight against it [public education] by all means in the name of God and the United States. You may, probably will be defeated. . . . The very defeat of the question will be a gain.

Even some New Yorkers evidenced confusion over the outcome of the controversy. In 1849, an upstater wrote Seward that the school question was not properly understood, "for there is an impression in certain quarters that the latter [Catholics] have privileges & advantages under the existing laws which are not enjoyed by the citizens generally." Seward's explanation was less colored and much more matter-of-fact than Hughes's analysis. As a privately controlled, though publicly supported, Protestant educational corporation, the Public School Society operated the city's schools "in such a way as to raise conscientious objections by the Catholics against the instruction given in the schools." As a result of this situation, "Catholics refused to send their children to the public schools and thus one-fourth or one-fifth of the children of New York were left to grow up without education." Since Seward regarded education as essential to the success of republican government, he offered his initial suggestion to subsidize Catholic schools, which was later amended to replace the Society with the state district system of schools:

> What was recommended was to let the Catholics support schools of their own and receive their own share of the public monies. What was *done* was to divide the city into school districts and let the schools be organized and conducted by trustees and a Board of Education elected by the People—without reference to religion. This is the new system. It is the same that always existed in the rural parts of the state. It immediately brought in the Catholic children. The abuse was a religious close monopoly of education with the public funds. The reform consists in having abolished the monopoly.

It is evident that the bishop and the former governor did not view the outcome in the same light. For Seward, New York's solution was an end; for Hughes, it was a midpoint. Since the district school system was an immense improvement over the Society and since the present number of Catholic schools was insufficient to provide an "exclusively Catholic training" for all the children of the diocese, Hughes felt "obliged to tolerate the attendance of our poor children at these schools until we should, with time and the blessing of Almighty God, be enabled to erect schools of our own for their exclusively Catholic training."

None of the protagonists in the controversy advocated religious indifferentism or secularism in the schools. Instead, the majority of Protestants advocated a nondenominational Christianity as the only compromise between "infidelity" and denominational instruction. In his *Public Schools and Moral Education,* Neil McCluskey convincingly argues that this "prin-

ciple turned out to be only a compromise, for the 'medium' between sectarianism and atheism became in practice a form of sectarianism which
did not long satisfy even the more liberal religious groups." It certainly
did not satisfy Hughes. Despite an impulsive and single-minded personality that often made him insensitive to the Protestant pulse of nineteenth-century America, Hughes realized that there was no such thing as
nonsectarian Christianity or undenominational religion. When nondenominationalism was taught, sectarianism was taught, regardless of the
brand or the label.

The Bible was a case in point. Both Catholics and Protestants accepted
the Bible as the word of God. But at this point a line of demarcation
appeared. Protestants read several versions and believed in private interpretation while Catholics insisted upon an authorized version of the Bible
approved by the authority of the Church. For Protestants, Bible reading
in the public schools without note or comment was a religious, or at least
a moral, act; for Catholics, this type of Scripture reading signified Protestant sectarianism. Yet even before the passage of the school bill, the new
state superintendent of common schools, Samuel Young, judged the "New
Testament as in all respects a suitable book to be daily read in our Common Schools, and I earnestly and cordially recommend its general introduction for this purpose." Under New York City's first superintendent of
schools, William Stone, staunch opponent of the Catholic school position
and editor of the *Commercial Advertiser,* and his successor, Meredith
Reese, public school Bible-reading became firmly entrenched. In opposition to Catholic objections, the Board of Education ruled in 1844 "that
the Bible without note or comment, at the opening of the schools is not
inculcating or practising any religious or sectarian doctrine or tenet of any
particular Christian or other religious sect."

Since Hughes believed that religion could never effectively be excluded
from the public schools and regarded religious neutrality as an illusion,
his first attempt was to de-Protestantize the public schools. He failed because the nondenominationalism which he denounced as sectarianism was
the compromise that Protestants believed successfully avoided sectarianism
and atheism. Once it became apparent that he would not be successful in
this task, he led a concerted effort to acquire public funds for his Catholic
schools as an alternative. Even though the district system was a vast improvement over the Public School Society, Hughes did not accept it as

the answer to the Catholic educational dilemma. In evaluating the advantages of the new school law to Catholics, the *Freeman's Journal* emphasized Hughes's position that "we have to consider more the evils from which it relieves us, than the positive benefits which it confers." But this negative victory was not the Catholic answer. Although Hughes permitted Catholic children to attend public schools, he viewed this situation as only a temporary measure. For nondenominationalism was solidly entrenched in the public schools, and Bible reading without note or comment was the order of the day. As late as 1862, Hughes informed an Irish audience in Cork that American public schools were still teaching religiously offensive material to Catholic children "by stealth. . . . We know and see the effect of the teaching at such schools. The children become irreverent and profane towards their parents. . . ."

As time went on, however, and a decreasing emphasis was given to religious instruction in the public schools, Hughes transferred his main volleys from an attack "on the sectarian bias of the public schools" to an emphasis on public school godlessness. Although he had accused the Society's schools of being dens of infidelity, emphasis upon "Godless education" in secularist public schools became the bishop's major theme in later years. He characterized the common school as a "dragon . . . devouring the hope of the country as well as religion." Scarcely able to control his contempt, Hughes denounced public education as equivalent to "Socialism, Red Republicanism, Universalism, Infidelity, Deism, Atheism, and Pantheism—anything, everything, except religionism and patriotism." Although this choice of epithets was unique to Hughes, he was not alone in pursuing this line of attack. His friend and former secretary, Bishop James Roosevelt Bayley of Newark, deplored the alleged practical results of a common school education:

> Experience has since shown that the new system . . . is one which, as excluding all religious instruction, is most fatal to the morals and religious principles of our children, and that our only resource is to establish schools of our own, where sound religious instruction shall be imparted at the same time with secular instruction. If we needed any evidence upon the matter it would be found in the conduct and behavior of those of our children who are educated under the Christian Brothers, when contrasted with those who are exposed to the pernicious influences of a public school.

In a harsh attack on public education, a committee at the First Plenary Council of Baltimore in 1852 diagnosed its disease as the "exclusion of all religion therefrom, in other words, its Godlessness." Thus, the public schools simply could not win. If they inculcated religious values, they were labeled as sectarian; if they excluded religion, they were branded as secularistic or atheistic.

Such colored descriptions by Hughes, Bayley, the First Plenary Council, and other Catholic ecclesiastics painted an extreme version of what eventuated as a common American-Catholic attitude toward public education. This severe censure also convinced many Protestants that the Catholic Church was a dangerous enemy pledged to destroy the American public school system. Certainly, Hughes stands out as a major figure who helped to inculcate this unfortunate attitude in many generations of American Protestants. Furthermore, his complaints about sectarian public schools made him as responsible as Horace Mann for the eventual secularization of public education. If Mann's non-sectarian compromise "set in motion a process which has resulted in the legal secularization of most modern public school education," then the New York bishop's logic necessarily made him an unwitting ally in this secularization process.

Although the *Freeman's Journal* waged continuous warfare against the public schools, especially during the 1850's, Hughes deliberately avoided all further public controversy over the school question. He had made up his mind that further agitation for public aid for Catholic schools was hopeless—notwithstanding the optimism exhibited in his reminiscences. Instead, he abandoned the public schools and decided to concentrate his efforts on building and developing his own parochial school system. Hughes publicized this decision in an article he wrote in December, 1849, for the *Freeman's Journal:* "How are we to provide for the Catholic education of our children? I answer: Not by agitating the questions of the constitutionality, legality or expediency of State schools. Let us leave these points to be settled by the politicians. . . . Let us leave the public schools to themselves." Certainly the time was right at midcentury. Just the previous year Pope Pius IX had urged all bishops to establish Catholic schools, while in 1850 New York was raised to an archdiocese and Hughes elevated to archbishop. All during the 1840's, Hughes had grappled with many important problems connected with the establishment of a parochial school system: financial support, control of school property, teaching personnel, and the publication of suitable textbooks for Catholic schools. Now the new archbishop could synthesize all of these factors into a carefully formulated policy; and in his Circular Letter of 1850, Hughes enunciated the classic formula for the erection of Catholic schools that has guided Catholic educational policy to the present time:

> It may not be out of place to urge upon you the necessity of providing for the primary education of your children, in connection with the principles of our holy religion. I think the time is almost come when it will be necessary to build the school-house first, and the church afterwards. Our fellow-citizens have adopted a system of general education which I fear will result in consequences, to a great extent, the reverse of those which are anticipated. They have attempted to divorce religion, under the plea of excluding the sectarianism from elementary education and literature. There are some who seem to apprehend great mischief to the State, if the children in our public schools should have an opportunity of learning the first elements of the Christian doctrine in connection with their daily lessons. Happily they require of us only to contribute our portion of the expense necessary for the support of this system. This, as good citizens, we are bound to do; especially as we are not compelled to send our children to such schools, to receive the doubtful equivalent which is to be given for the taxes collected. I hope that the friends of education may not be disappointed in their expectations of benefits from this system, whilst for myself, I may be allowed to say that I do not regard it as suited to a Christian land, whether Catholic or Protestant, however admirably it might be adapted to the social condition of an enlightened paganism.

Hughes lost no time in promulgating this dictum and had it immediately codified into diocesan legislation: "Let parochial schools be established and maintained everywhere; the days have come, and the place, in which the school is more necessary than the church." Before the archbishop appointed a new pastor for a church, he charged him to "proceed upon the principle that, in this age and country, the school is before the church." Eminently a man of action, Hughes caused this policy to have effective results. By 1854, the number of Catholic schools had increased to twenty-eight and had instructed 10,061 pupils. Three years later the number of Catholic-school students climbed to 12,938, and by 1862, two years before his death, Hughes could boast that 15,000 Catholic youngsters were receiving a Catholic education in his diocese. To staff his expanding school system, he invited various religious teaching orders to implement their educational commitment in New York. The Religious of the Sacred Heart, the Jesuits, the Christian Brothers, the Sisters of Mercy, the Ursulines, the Sisters of Notre Dame, and the Sisters of the Good Shepherd all accepted Hughes's call.

During the early 1850's, Catholics in many different states struggled to obtain public funds for their schools. When all of these efforts proved fruitless, as Hughes no doubt knew they would, an increasing number of bishops concluded that the only alternative was to develop their own systems of education. Hughes's efforts in New York impressed other bishops, and they looked to his experience to help them in their own attempts to establish diocesan parochial school systems. Before long, school building programs were under way in the Catholic dioceses of Baltimore, Pittsburgh, Chicago, Cincinnati, Boston, and Philadelphia. Under Hughes's initial impetus and later educational legacy after his death in 1864, the collective body of Catholic bishops gradually promulgated progressively more stringent regulations concerning the establishment and organization of parochial schools. In a period of less than forty years—a period which witnessed the Know-Nothing excess, the Civil War and Reconstruction efforts, and the rapid transformation of American society—a separate system of Catholic schools began to emerge and develop parallel to the generally established public school system.

The First Plenary Council of Baltimore (1852) urged the bishops "to see that schools are established in connection with the churches of their dioceses" while the Second Provincial Council (1866), stressing the religious indifferentism of the increasingly secularistic public schools, repeated this admonition and pressed "Pastors to apply their efforts in accord with their resources to construct Parochial Schools, wherever it can be done." Finally, in 1884, the Third Plenary Council removed all options from both clergy and laity. Bishops and priests were no longer urged, but rather required, to build parochial schools; and laymen were no longer admonished to send their children to Catholic schools, but were bound to do so unless a bishop granted an exception for a serious cause. "Having carefully investigated all these [educational] matters," the council solemnly decreed that "Near each church, where it does not exist, a parochial school is to be erected within two years from the promulgation of this Council, and it is to be maintained in perpetuum, unless the Bishop, on account of grave difficulties, judges that a postponement may be allowed." In less than sixty years, the American Catholic hierarchy's idealism of 1829, its insistence in 1840 that "we are always better pleased to have a separate system of education for our children," and its constant admonitions in 1852 and 1866 to establish parochial schools were finally translated into official Catholic policy and legislation in 1884.

The school controversy in New York had convinced Hughes that Catholic educational needs could only be met by establishing a system of diocesan parochial schools. When other bishops failed in their quest for public school funds, they began to follow Hughes's lead in developing parochial schools. The American hierarchy finally legislated parochial schools for the entire American Catholic Church in 1884—nearly half a century after Hughes had decided to chart this educational course. Although frequently blustery, rash, and reckless, Hughes played a major role in planting the parochial school idea that blossomed into the legislation of 1884. "After 1840, when attempts to gain public support for New York parochial schools failed" declares McCluskey, "Catholic interest and energy began to be expended almost exclusively on Catholic parochial and private schools, leaving the public schools as a semi-Protestant domain." As a result, many Catholic authors have honored Hughes as the father of Catholic education in America. If this be so, then it is paradoxical that the father of American Catholic education should also have acted as a catalyst in the eventual secularization of American public education.

Irish Catholic Life in
Yankee City

STEPHAN THERNSTROM

The overwhelming mass of American Catholics in the nineteenth century were immigrants. They were humble people who left few written descriptions of their daily life and whose history is obscure. Their descendants today often know little more than that their forefathers were poor, struggled hard, and gradually fought their way up in the world. The following selection provides a brief glimpse of what this kind of life was like. It is taken from Stephan Thernstrom's *Poverty and Progress* (1964), a study of social mobility in Newburyport, Massachusetts, the community made famous by W. Lloyd Warner's anthropological studies of "Yankee City." Mr. Thernstrom, who is Professor of History at University of California at Los Angeles, points out the connection between the growing size, wealth, and status of the Catholic group in Newburyport, and their acceptance of American attitudes and values.

T HE CATHOLIC CHURCH CAME TO NEWBURYPORT WITH THE NEW working class, and the story of its growing strength and its gradual and hesitant acceptance by the Protestant majority is also the story of the integration of the new working class into the community. To many troubled citizens of Newburyport at mid-century, the alien newcomers formed an isolated, atomized mass, detached from and hostile to the community. By 1880 great numbers of these workmen, now industrious,

Reprinted by permission of the publishers from Stephan Thernstrom, *Poverty and Progress: Social Mobility in a 19th Century City,* pp. 171-180. Cambridge, Mass.: Harvard University Press, Copyright, 1964, by the President and Fellows of Harvard College.

home-loving citizens, were identified as devout members of a church which had been "Americanized" and was clearly in Newburyport to stay. The Church of Immaculate Conception was welcomed by few Yankees, but by 1880 it was widely tolerated as a lesser evil. Whatever the religious reservations of the Protestant majority, the powerfully conservative social influence of Catholicism was coming to be appreciated. A Newburyport attorney summed up the new attitude crudely and effectively when he remarked: "When we pull down a Catholic church, we must put up a penitentiary."

Both the Irish and their church encountered suspicion and some hostility in Newburyport in their first years there. Little can be learned about the activities of the Newburyport Catholic community in the 1850's. Special religious events—communion ceremonies, Easter services—occasionally received mention in the local press, but rarely anything more. No Irish or Catholic groups participated in the massive Fourth of July celebration in 1854. The newcomers were distinctly outsiders. When they offended some tenet of Yankee morality it was a matter for public concern; otherwise they were ignored. Not until it sponsored a public lecture by the famous Irish-American orator Thomas d'Arcy McGee was the Independent Benevolent Society, "a society of . . . foreign residents, who associate for intellectual and moral improvement and for pecuniary aid and assistance in sickness and distress," referred to in the local paper.

This lonely item appeared in 1856. Contrast with it an ordinary newsnote from the 1870's. The local priest, Father A. J. Teeling, was leaving the city for a visit to Europe; the Catholic community held a farewell gathering for him and presented him with a gift of $1000. The roster of sponsoring organizations read as follows: The Men's Sodality, The Holy Name, The Married Ladies' Sodality, The Young Ladies' Sodality, The Rosary, The Church Choir, The Catholic Battalion, The Holy Angels' Sodality, The Society of the Infant Jesus, and The Ancient Order of Hibernians! Music was provided by the Catholic Band. The energies of this multitude of Irish associations were conspicuously demonstrated in the great Saint Patrick's Day parades of the seventies; the sympathetic reporting these received in the press suggests something of the new status of the Irish in the community. As many as a thousand sons of Erin usually turned out for the proceedings. Men of the Father Lennon Benevolent Society appeared resplendent in hats with green ostrich plumes, sashes trimmed with a silver fringe, white belts, and dark suits. Gaudily uniformed Hibernians displayed a large and costly silk banner depicting Saint Patrick banishing the snakes, as well as a gigantic American flag. The Catholic Church could claim the allegiance of a quarter of the Newburyport population by 1880; no wonder that the mayor and the City Council saw fit to march with the priest at the head of the Saint Patrick's Day processions. Nor did the determination to build parochial schools arouse violent opposition; the 1880 Catholic Fair to raise funds for that purpose was attended by the Mayor, the aldermen, the School Committee members, and several Protestant leaders, including a Congregational minister.

The subsidence of Know-Nothing fears and the growing acceptance of the Catholic population was partly a result of the Civil War. The crisis of the Union heightened common loyalties and dissolved many of the suspicions of the fifties. The war seemed no respecter of persons; local men fought and died "independent of rank, of office, of social position." The problem of how to "weld all the conflicting and discordant elements" of the community into "one compact body" had once appeared almost insoluble, declaimed the Memorial Day orator. "No prophet's voice could foretell" that the war would act as a "mighty furnace" in which these "discordant elements were melted and moulded into one organic whole." The Irish proved eager recruits and able soldiers. One of them later boasted that his countrymen were Americans twice over—"by their oath under the law, and by their sword in the war."

If local Irishmen were proving themselves true Americans on the battlefield, their church was proving itself American in its devotion to property and free competition. The Catholicism the immigrant brought to the New World was a fatalistic peasant religion which sharply conflicted with the optimistic, expansionist assumptions of American social thought of the age. Clerics who could write that "in more than 99 cases in a 100 we shall have reason to rejoice if the son turns out as well as the father" were challenging the essence of the ideology of mobility, as were the Italian Catholics whose view of worldly success was that well-to-do Protestants "were under the most especial protection of the devil, who fattened them in this world that they might burn better in the next." The clash between these opposing world views was undoubtedly one source of the Know-Nothing protest in the fifties. But the speed with which the Catholic world view accommodated itself to American conditions was impressive. In Newburyport Catholicism was well on its way to being "Americanized" within a generation of its establishment.

Reverend Henry Lennon, the local parish priest from 1848 to 1871, and his successor, Reverend A. J. Teeling, were builders. They were dedicated to accumulating property as well as to saving souls, and they saw clearly that a thrifty, hard-working, well-educated congregation would contribute to that end. As early as 1853 Father Lennon won the praise of the managers of the Free Evening School for his support: "Father Lennon is always ready to assist in a good work, and especially in those matters that tend to elevate his own people, for whose advancement in this city his labors are untiring." A dramatic action taken by the priest in the financial crisis of 1857 showed his control over his flock working to the advantage of the community. According to local legend, still repeated twenty years later, the decisive factor in halting a disastrous run on the savings bank was Father Lennon's advice to his congregation to leave their deposits untouched. The Church of the Immaculate Conception was mortgaged for $8000 at that time, and the priest is supposed to have announced: "You call for your money from the savings bank; the bank forecloses the mortgage on us; I call for the money from you and pay it over and the bank has the money and you have paid at once, with hardship, a debt which spread over some years, would have been easy to bear."

The struggle to build church facilities out of the slender earnings of an almost exclusively working class congregation was exceptionally difficult in the 1850's. As savings began to mount in the sixties and seventies, and as a small group of Catholic businessmen and professionals emerged, larger sums poured into church coffers. In 1874 alone $17,000 was devoted to improving the Green Street structure and to acquiring additional real estate. Between 1871 and 1879 Newburyport Catholics gave an estimated $65,000 for the maintenance, improvement, and expansion of church property.

The financial sacrifices made by Newburyport Catholics were impressive testimony to their religious dedication. A list of donors of $50 or more to a special fund drive in 1879 included some two dozen ordinary laborers from the mobility sample. Those were enormous sums to come from men earning little more than a dollar a day, of course, and they suggest a necessary qualification to the broadly correct conclusion that "it is difficult to distinguish the Irish drive to advance the cause of the Church from the drive for social status." True, the church prospered as its communicants prospered. True, the Catholic workman derived status from his identification with the largest and most rapidly growing church in the community. But the fact remains that the church was a heavy drain on resources which, from the point of view of worldly success, might have been put to more productive uses. It has already been demonstrated that the Irish working class families of Newburyport, though more successful at accumulating property than their native counterparts, were markedly less mobile in the occupational sphere. The financial sacrifices the Irish made to further their religion may have had an effect similar to that of their drive for home ownership. Both promoted maximum concentration on immediate accumulation, and discouraged such long-term investments as higher education or even apprenticeship for one's children. A perceptive observer of the Irish community in New York concludes that the development of solid middle class dynasties among Irish Catholics was inhibited by the fact that "a good part of the surplus that might have gone into family property has gone to building the church." For the Catholic workmen of Newburyport the point is slightly different, for these men accumulated more family property than Yankees of similar occupational status and gave heavily to the church as well. It was rather that both the land hunger and the religious devotion of the working class Catholic led him to seek property at the cost of education and the forms of mobility which required education.

Some of the Newburyport Irish, of course, did manage to climb out of the working class. The emergence of a small elite of Catholic businessmen and professionals in the sixties and seventies, some of them recruited from the ranks of labor, was of great significance. This group of successful men of property shared the prudent conservatism of the local priesthood. While the great majority of the Newburyport Catholic population was working class, the leadership of the elaborate network of church-related social organizations came largely from the business class. The key figures in the Father Lennon Benevolent Society in 1871, for example, were mostly businessmen. Through their control of the voluntary associations, respectable and successful men such as these acted both as models for their ethnic group, and as mediators between it and the larger community. The career of John Quill, prominent in several of these societies, illustrates the point well. Quill opened a grocery near the waterfront in the early fifties, and carried on a thriving business until his death in 1880. He served as a financial counselor and general adviser to a good many of his countrymen; the records of the Institution for Savings show that illiterate Irish depositors usually brought either the priest or John Quill to sign the account book for them. The *Herald* noted Quill's passing with an editorial praising his beneficial influence on the local Irish and concluding: "He was very well educated, and a worthy and honest man, who had the respect of all who knew him."

The respect won by "worthy and honest" Catholic men of property like John Quill, Patrick Henry, and Hugh McGlew did not, of course, signify a complete reversal in the attitudes of the Protestant majority toward Catholicism. A speech given in Newburyport in 1880 denounced all Catholics as "political and ecclesiastical tools of the Roman priesthood," and declared that the power of the Church in America was a clear violation of the Monroe Doctrine. The *Herald* editor brooded over the fact that Catholics, only a quarter of the population of New England, accounted for three quarters of the births; a correspondent offered the consolation that infant mortality was exceptionally high among the impoverished Catholic masses. The newspaper took a perverse pleasure in the prospect that the successor to the dying Pius IX would likely be reactionary: "The more reactionary the result of the election, the better for the cause of progress and civilization. There is nothing better for the right and the truth than the baldest and boldest advocacy of the wrong and the false."

Despite the gains which had been made since the fifties, in 1880 Newburyport was still a divided community, and it appeared likely to remain so. The division, however, was not the simple class division of "have-alls" and "lack-alls" that loomed on the horizon at mid-century. Religious and ethnic differences had outweighed class considerations. The large Irish, Roman Catholic component of the working class was securely attached to a church and a church-related associational structure dominated by a priest and a business elite firmly committed to the prevailing American ideology of enterprise and success. The Catholics of Newburyport, a fourth of the population in 1880 and destined to increase further with continuing immigration, were set off from the rest of the community in many ways. The elaborate organizational structure which had grown up by then was designed to meet all the social needs of the Catholic population, and it provided a series of "structural fences . . . contrived to keep the ethnic individual articulated to the church and the community while keeping him from straying too far out" into the community social system. The parochial schools established in Newburyport in 1882 were the capstone of this system.

The integration of the Catholic population into the larger community, therefore, was partial, and the attitude of the community was accordingly a blend of hostility and approval. The Catholic Church was "aggressive, temporizing, and deceitful," but it was by no means "an unmitigated evil." Religious objections and mistrust of Catholic separatism competed with appreciation of the church as an instrument of discipline and control over "the dangerous classes." A deeply ambivalent editorial on the problem summed up the sentiment which had come to prevail by 1880: "There is not a reasonable person in the town, who employs a Catholic girl in his family, who would not prefer one devoted to her religion, constant at church . . . When they deny their religion they seldom accept ours, but that class furnish the night walkers, the drunkards and the criminals."

German Catholics and the Nationality Controversy

COLMAN J. BARRY, O.S.B.

Besides the Irish, the other major immigrant component in nineteenth-century American Catholicism was German. The quarrels between these two elements were legendary. Sometimes nothing more than local manifestations of ethnic jealousy were involved, but in the 1880s and 1890s the "nationality question" became a very serious matter. The controversy that developed then was sometimes described as springing from "Cahenslyism" because of the role played by a German merchant named Peter Paul Cahensly. But it is more accurately thought of as a controversy over Americanization, for the underlying issue concerned the kind of adjustments Catholicism should make in this new social and political environment. Colman J. Barry, O.S.B., author of several books on Catholic history and now President of St. John's University in Collegeville, Minnesota, devoted a volume to the nationality question in 1953. Here he summarizes his findings in an essay first published in 1960.

T HE CATHOLIC CHURCH IN THE UNITED STATES HAS BEEN IN large measure an immigrant institution. The tide of immigration which brought millions of settlers to American shores created a phenomenon for this Church which was unparalleled in its history. Peoples of different races and nationalities, of distinct traditions and prejudices, came individually or in groups to establish new homes in a strange country. Among these varied nationalities the German people occupied a leading place. Immigrant German Catholics of the nineteenth century had a firm loyalty to their religion, sound organizational techniques, and a strong community pattern of worship, culture and social action. From the time of their first Pennsylvania settlements in the mid-eighteenth century, German Catholic leaders had insisted on separate treatment and recognition as a minority group. Their demands in the following century for language rights, national parishes, and proportional representation in the hierarchy were, they maintained, defenses against attack by liberal German Americans after 1848, as well as insurance that their religious faith would be preserved intact.

Simultaneously, leading Catholic churchmen and laymen, following the pioneer example of the first Catholic bishop of the United States, John Carroll, of the colonial Maryland Carroll family, were working to instill devotion to American constitutional and political ideals among immigrant Catholics. Towards the end of the century differences over procedure and practice brought robust Americanizing and German elements into an open conflict. German Catholic leaders and newspapers, supported by a large number of French, Polish, and Spanish representatives both in the United States and abroad, accused the Americanizers of striving to break down in a precipitate fashion all traditions and customs among Catholic immigrants. The Americanizers were also accused of causing a loss of religious faith and creating an undue attachment to American secular trends.

On their side the Americanizers, following especially the principles of Orestes Brownson and Isaac Hecker, were wedded to the vision of traditional Catholicism formed in an American democratic mold, and based on a fusion of all national groups. They maintained that free political institutions can be secure only when the people are imbued with religious ideals, that without the religious sanctions so indispensable to democracy, the moral solidarity which makes democratic government possible would be broken. Like Lacordaire, Schlegel, and Wiseman had done in Europe, they wanted to show the necessity of the Catholic religion to the modern world and to impress on Catholics the necessity of their being in tune with the age. Foremost in the ranks of the Americanizers were James Cardinal Gibbons, Archbishop of Baltimore; Archbishop John Ireland of St. Paul, who had been called "the consecrated blizzard of the northwest"; Bishop John J. Keane, rector of the Catholic University of America, and later archbishop of Dubuque; Bishop Denis J. O'Connell, rector of the American College in Rome; the Society of St. Paul the Apostle, or Paulists, which Isaac Hecker had founded; and the majority of the professors at the Catholic University of America in Washington.

This task of creating a religious and national unity among the Catholic immigrants reached a climax during the years after the War Between the States to World War I. German immigration to the United States was given a new impetus after 1865, and Catholics made up an average of over thirty-five per cent of the total German immigration of that period. They totaled around 700,000 in number during the period 1865 to 1900, and became the largest Catholic immigrant group arriving in the States. Between 1830–1870 Irish immigrants had come in largest numbers, up to fifty per cent above the German totals. But by 1865 the Germans had equalled the Irish influx and, from 1870–1890, the Germans led the field until Italian immigration began in earnest in the last decade of the century, and continued as the dominant immigrant movement for many years.

The rapid recovery of the North after 1865, and the advancement of world communication encouraged this movement of Germans to America. But conditions in Germany itself were, perhaps, a more influential factor in this new and larger tide of immigration. The movement toward unification of the German peoples entailed in its wake political conditions which drove many citizens from their homeland. When heavier taxes and universal military service became the keynote of the new regime, especially after the rise to power of Count Otto von Bismarck; when the small landowners, farm hands, domestic hand workers and shop keepers found they had to abandon their traditional ways of life in a new military-industrial society—many saw their only hope of self-sufficiency and independence in emigration. But more important than these factors for the Catholics of Germany, perhaps, was the *Kulturkampf*. This religious persecution, which reached its peak in Falk's May Laws of 1873, practically annulled papal jurisdiction over German Catholics, abolished religious orders, and fined and deposed resisting German bishops. Although Catholics of the Rhine provinces, Bavaria, and Prussian Poland combined under the leadership of Ludwig Windthorst to wage the Center Party's campaign of "passive resistance," many priests and nuns were forced to flee. A large number of Germany's Catholic laity, wearied by the campaign of vilification in newspapers, and the constant pressure against their faith by their political masters, also turned their eyes toward foreign lands, especially the United States. In 1883 an agent of the *St. Raphaelsverein* in Hamburg asked a Catholic tenant from the Rhineland why he and his family were emigrating to America. He answered:

> My landlord gave us free lodging and 23-30 pfennig a day for wages. For this my whole family had to labor on Sundays as well as weekdays. We were obliged to do our own chores during free hours and on Sunday afternoons. If we asked permission to go to Church on Sunday, the man then abused us . . . every time and said: "You won't always have to be running after the priest if you find yourselves in the alms house." And so I am going to America. My friends write from there that they have such good conditions, and on Sundays as many as want to may go to Church. My children shall not imitate my slavery!

Germans who came after 1865 generally settled in the same regions as earlier German immigrants. As in the eighteenth and early nineteenth centuries German settlers had chosen the best farming land they could find, so in the last half of the nineteenth century they settled in agricultural and metropolitan areas which in time became known as "the German belt." This zone lay between the northern boundaries of Massachusetts and of Maryland, spread westward through the Ohio river basin to the Great Lakes, and then out into the prairie states beyond the Mississippi river. Germans settled in the Mohawk Valley, eastern Pennsylvania, along the shores of the Ohio and Great Lakes, and down the Mississippi to New Orleans. But it was in the triangle embracing Cincinnati, Milwaukee and St. Louis that the German population was especially dense.

Catholic Germans were concerned not only with their material well-being in the new world, but primarily with their spiritual life. This may be deduced from the fact that among their first interests was the erection of a church and a parish school. Fresh from Germany and feeling isolated because of their language differences, the German Catholics from the out-set insisted that separate churches were an absolute necessity for them-selves. They settled together in colonies whenever possible, often by their own choice, more often under the direction of a German priest or mission-ary. They desired to have churches of their own in which their traditional religious observances and customs could be carried out, where they could hear sermons in their mother tongue, go to confession as they had learned

which we Catholics, as a body, are regarded by the people of this country only as a sort of foreign camp in their midst, who will in time scatter
and be lost in the mass of the Protestant, or at least non-Catholic population. Though the census will show that the Catholic far exceeds the foreign population, only part of which is Catholic, it is not easy to convince
or disabuse them. Many things which they see and know, keep up the
delusion. A Protestant will point to the map and say: "Where are your
American Catholics? The whole country is laid off in dioceses, as though
you owned it, but how is it that your Popes have never found an American Catholic fit to occupy a see west of the Mississippi and Lake St.
Clair? There are thousands of miles where no American-born bishop has
ever been seen."

Two German priests of St. Louis, Wilhelm Faerber and Ignatius Wapel-
horst, were not slow to take up these charges, and in a German-Catholic
theological monthly, *Das Pastoral Blatt,* they branded Shea's article as
Nativism and Know-Nothingism. They also charged him with insulting
prelates who had labored amid unspeakable hardships when no native-
born priests could be found in the West. They insisted that Germans always adapted themselves very quickly to a new environment and added:

> Let us allow things quietly to take their course, and to develop them-
> selves in a natural manner. How in the future the different nationalities
> will unite harmoniously in one people, what is to become of the different
> languages, of the German churches and schools, will all be arranged later
> on. Forcible, premature interference is always dangerous. "In nature there
> is no leap"; this also holds good in the development of things social,
> political, and religious. Let us cheerfully permit our descendants to settle
> those questions. When once immigration has entirely ceased, and there
> lives a generation that has been reared up with its priests, the English
> language will also be gradually adopted in the churches.

German Catholic leaders in the St. Louis area began at once to apply
these principles in practice. They challenged Archbishop Kenrick's policy
in regard to German, Bohemian, and Polish congregations in that jurisdiction. Kenrick held, because the decrees of the Council of Trent had been
promulgated in the territory of the Louisiana Purchase, that these parishes
did not enjoy all the rights and privileges of English-speaking parishes.
They were succursal churches for the use of their respective nationalities,
and that in one given territory there was to be one parish church, namely
the English-speaking church, despite the fact that the German congregations were larger and more active than any other parishes of the area.

They began a press compaign for equality, and eighty-two priests sent a petition to the Propaganda Congregation in Rome which had been prepared by the Vicar General of St. Louis, Heinrich Muehlsiepen. Faerber went to Rome to push the petition personally. Cardinal Simeoni, Prefect of Propaganda, referred the petition to the archbishops of the United States for their opinions, and it was in this way that they heard of it for the first time. Cardinal Gibbons told Simeoni that the matter would be discussed at the forthcoming Third Plenary Council of Baltimore in 1884, and he assigned it to the Committee on New Business, composed of Archbishops Williams of Boston, Feehan of Chicago and Heiss of Milwaukee. He stated that he did this because the archbishop of Milwaukee could then have a voice in the discussion. But this committee reported nothing to the floor on the St. Louis petition, and the Germans present remained silent on the subject throughout all executive and public sessions. When German Catholics continued to question this lack of action, Gibbons was not slow to point out that the German leaders present had initiated no discussion when the opportunity was offered to them.

Bishops Gilmour of Cleveland and Moore of St. Augustine took the decrees of this council to Rome for approval, and there they found that petitions and letters had been coming from German Catholics in the United States requesting Rome to safeguard their interests from the aggressions of English-speaking and Irish Catholics. These two bishops prepared a memorial of their own in which they claimed that a spirit of nationalism was being introduced by deliberate effort, that a conflict would result with consequent loss to religion, while Catholics of all nationalities would become ridiculous in the eyes of the non-Catholic population of the United States. If the Germans formed themselves into a distinct nationalizing movement it would be more harmful to their Church than a renewal of the Know-Nothing attacks of thirty years previous.

But almost immediately another organized protest was made in the Milwaukee sector of the "German triangle." After the Baltimore council the Vicar General of Milwaukee, Peter Abbelen, prepared a petition, signed by Archbishop Heiss, which he brought to Rome. Its arguments were strikingly similar to those from St. Louis; he asked Rome to stop forcible Americanization on the part of priests and bishops. But this time the leader among the Americanizers, Archbishop Ireland, was himself on the scene. He and Bishop Keane were at that time in England, on their way to Rome to make arrangements for the founding of the Catholic University of America. When Monsignor O'Connell at the American College informed them by cable of Abbelen's mission they rushed to Rome and the issue was squarely met. They found that a number of curia cardinals were exercising a powerful influence in favor of the Germans. They were the Church historian, Josef Cardinal Hergenroether; the Jesuit, Johann Cardinal Franzelin, and two exiled German archbishops, victims of Bismarck's *Kulturkampf*, Paulus Cardinal Melchers, archbishop of Cologne, and Miecislaus Cardinal Ledochowski, archbishop of Gnesen-Posen. They found that the impression at the Propaganda had been at first entirely in Abbelen's favor, and that it had been proposed to appoint a cardinal protector for the German Catholics in the United States. Ireland and Keane presented a lengthy document to the Propaganda, asking for a delay until the American bishops could be heard. They won their point, and then proceeded to cable all of the archbishops and several bishops at home, warning them of the demands the Germans were making. Gibbons summoned a meeting of the archbishops at Philadelphia so they could, as he said, "state our side of the question, as the German bishops have (surreptitiously) already stated theirs." They forwarded on the next mail boat to Rome a defense of their administration, insisted they were not uprooting old-world customs, but that the process of Americanization had already begun and they were determined that Catholics be a part of it. Many individual bishops sent letters: in one Bishop Gilmour of Cleveland wanted the matter taken directly to Pope Leo XIII, and he declared if something were not done, "within twenty-five years the Church in the Mississippi valley would be bound hand and foot to the wheel of Germanism." Bishop William McCloskey declared:

> If these German prelates are allowed special legislation as Germans, great injury is likely to follow to the interests of religion. We will be looked upon as a German Church in an English-speaking country. Let the Italians fancy a German element in the Church of Italy, riding rough shod over the Italians. How would your Cardinals and the Pope fancy it?

The Congregation of Propaganda gave its decision the following June: since the bishops had been establishing parishes for the respective language groups, the Germans should not demand further privileges; that local bishops should decide whether English or German be used in individual parishes, and that any person had the right to choose an English-speaking parish after he had reached the age of maturity, if he should so desire.

The Americanizers were jubilant that they had won this point, and despite a hot press and pamphlet campaign that was continued by both sides, the matter was terminated at this point.

The German question then took on a second, and quite different, character. For some years a German Catholic layman of extraordinary vision had been working for the spiritual and material welfare of Catholic immigrants as they left European ports. This man, Peter Paul Cahensly, a merchant of Limburg an der Lahn, while pursuing his commercial interests at Hamburg, Bremen, and LeHavre, had become conscious of the thousands of Germans who were leaving these ports for North and South America. After long, tiresome low-class rail journeys, these people arrived exhausted and frightened in a strange port city, such as LeHavre, without knowledge of the French language. Cahensly watched them fall into the hands of unscrupulous agents, landlords and innkeepers who tricked and robbed them. With the support of the archbishop of Rouen, Henri Bonnechose, he established his first immigrant hotel at LeHavre, persuaded a religious order to take charge, and then began to examine conditions on board ships carrying immigrants to the new world. He made two trips incognito in steerage to Baltimore and New York and recorded his impressions:

A person could climb only with the greatest difficulty to the upper and rear places because of the small amount of free space which was usually barricaded with boxes and trunks. Besides, almost total darkness existed, and I became frightened when I thought that in these small rooms of indescribable disorder and darkness hundreds of people should spend weeks and months. By dividing the sleeping places, difference of sex was almost completely neglected, and it is not surprising that under such circumstances immoral situations developed which defy description.

Cahensly resolved to present his case before the yearly assembly of Catholic societies of Germany, known as the *Katholikentag*. In a short time he had secured official support from the German hierarchy, financial help from the Catholic laity, and a *St. Raphaelsverein* for the protection of German Catholic immigrants was established under the presidency of Prince Karl Isenburg-Birstein of Offenbach. They requested companies such as the *Nord Deutscher Lloyd* to establish immigration regulations, petitioned the French and Belgian governments to set up port authorities, erected immigrant missions at Bremen, Hamburg, Antwerp and LeHavre. They petitioned President Grant to initiate an international immigration commission, and sent a memorial to each of the American Catholic bishops asking them to take an interest in the needs of immigrants and to support their movement. They received no answers from the United States, nor from their own German government, which looked upon emigration as unpatriotic desertion of the fatherland. The government opened a press campaign against the *St. Raphaelsverein,* imprisoned several of their agents, and branded the whole movement as a Catholic effort to spirit their numbers out of Germany. Cahensly was elected a member of the Prussian House of Representatives, and later of the *Reichstag,* and strove through the Center Party to initiate emigration legislation, which the government successfully defeated year after year until 1907, when the Emigration Law of that year came too late to help the large majority of German emigrants.

Pope Leo XIII, however, encouraged Cahensly in his efforts, bestowed honors upon him, and suggested to him that the movement be broadened on an international base. Austrian, Italian, Swiss, Spanish and French St. Raphael Societies were accordingly founded, and Cahensly made a trip to the United States in 1883 to organize an American branch of the movement to help immigrants when they arrived in American ports. This St. Raphael movement, which began in 1865 and continues today, is a most interesting study in international social action and cooperation, supported entirely by free-will offerings and it seems the first such organized effort in modern times. By 1913 there were 109 St. Raphael agents operating throughout the world: fifteen in Europe, fourteen in Canada, three in Argentina, twenty-two in Brazil, seventeen in Uruguay, twelve each in Africa and Australia, two in Chile, one each in Mexico and Peru, and twenty in the United States.

The St. Raphael immigration movement became a part of the nationality question in the United States in an interesting manner. Cahensly had requested the German Catholics of America to support the movement. After the first rebuff of the St. Louis and Milwaukee petitions, the German Catholic bishops and priests had organized themselves into a *Deutsch-*

Amerikaner Priester-Verein, began yearly meetings to pursue their interests, and organized with the German Catholic laity, a yearly American *Katholikentag* as a manifestation of their solidarity and purpose. This movement was looked upon with serious misgivings by American Catholics, and when these German unions swung behind Cahensly a second conflict emerged. Collections were made throughout the United States to erect the Leo House on West 23rd Street in New York to care for incoming immigrants, guide them on their journey, and direct them to Catholic colonies in the West. What was an international movement at its base thus became in the United States a part of the Germanizing effort. Accordingly, when fifty-one representatives of the St. Raphael societies from seven nations met in Lucerne in December of 1890, and submitted a memorial to Rome asking for definite rights for Catholic immigrants, it was interpreted in the United States as another movement for German particularism. The Lucerne memorialists asked for separate churches for each nationality, priests of the same nationality as their congregations, instruction in the mother tongues, separate parochial schools for each nationality, equal rights for each nationality, and most important of all, proportional representation in the hierarchy for each nationality. Monsignor O'Connell at the American College again warned Archbishop Ireland of what was going on, and together they worked through their friends in the Associated Press to publicize the movement as a German plot by issuing cables to the press from Berlin. Archbishop Ireland also called in the reporters, branded the movement as "Cahenslyism," and forcefully declared:

> What is the most strange feature in this whole Lucerne movement is the impudence of these men in undertaking to meddle under any pretext in the Catholic affairs of America. This is simply unpardonable and all American Catholics will treasure up the affront for future action. We acknowledge the Pope of Rome as our chieftain in spiritual matters and we are glad to receive directions from him, but men in Germany or Switzerland or Ireland must mind their own business and be still as to ours.
>
> Nor is this the most irritating fact in this movement. The inspiration of the work in Europe comes, the dispatch tells us, from a clique in America . . .
>
> Our bishops will be chosen for their offices without regard to their race or their birthplace. The condition for their elevation being their

fitness, and for this fitness two things will be required: that they be strong in Catholicity and strong in Americanism.

Indeed, Mr. Cahensly and his supporters are somewhat excusable when they see in Americans naught else, or little else, than foreigners or foreign dominations. This is largely, they perceive, the case in politics. Why should it not be, they ask, in religion? When we will be more American in civil and political matters, there will be fewer petitions from vereins in America and from conferences in Lucerne for the foreignizing of Catholics in America.

The words of the archbishop of St. Paul on this occasion, as on so many others, evoked warm support from non-Catholics. The Lucerne Memorial became an issue of national importance, and the press of the nation discussed it, pro and con, while Catholics took sides to such an extent that Cardinal Gibbons declared it was "his greatest battle." He was determined that the Catholic Church would continue homogeneous like the nation. He was firmly convinced that nationalist groups in the Church would tend to become political elements. He deprecated the introduction of foreign nationalism and class voting into national politics. He, and the other Americanizers were close friends of Theodore Roosevelt, Senator Albert Beveridge of Indiana, William McKinley and Benjamin Harrison, and were part of the movement toward American national consciousness that was taking over the center of the stage in national life. The newer immigrant groups, like the Germans, did not participate at once and so readily in this growing vision of the so-called "inevitable destiny" of the American people. German Catholics in particular had grown accustomed in Germany to look upon their government as oppressive, liberal, and anti-religious, and carried that same prejudice with them to the new world.

A large majority of American bishops began writing to Rome in protest against the memorial, and insisted that Gibbons assemble a refutation and write directly to the Pope. The cardinal was vacationing at Cape May, N. J., at the time, and while returning along the boardwalk one day he met President Harrison who invited him to stop at his cottage. There the President discussed the Lucerne Memorial at length with Gibbons, congratulated him on the public stand he had taken against it, said he would have made a public statement himself seconding Gibbons' refutation but was afraid he would be accused of interfering in church matters. He told the Cardinal that he felt the United States was no longer a missionary country, and of all men the bishops of the church should be in full harmony with the political institutions and sentiments of the country. Gibbons was not slow to report this conversation to the papal secretary of state, Mario Cardinal Rampolla. The decision of Rome on the Lucerne petition had already been sent, however, and it was exactly as the Americanizers desired. Leo XIII had stated that the plan was neither opportune nor necessary, and that existing procedures would continue according to the proposals of the national episcopate.

Archbishop Ireland was pleased, but at the same time determined to make a national issue of the affair. He asked his good friend Senator Cushman Kellogg Davis, Republican Senator from Minnesota, to deliver a speech on the floor of the Senate against foreign interference in American life. Davis did this on April 22, 1892, and branded the Lucerne Memorial as a prostitution of religious power to political purposes, while making a personal attack on Cahensly as a tool of the German government.

It is on this point specifically that an acquittal is owed in simple justice. To attack Cahensly without checking or at least giving an ear to his clear denials of having arranged a plot; to release manufactured news releases in which his name was associated with a conspiracy; to coin a phrase, playing upon the name of a man who had worked as a pioneer in international social work among immigrants before any American bishops or societies had inaugurated such activity; to associate political intrigue of a Pan-German character with a man who had been at odds since 1871 with his own government over immigrant care—only reveal the emotional intensity of the controversy of these years. At the same time the Lucerne Memorialists cannot be exonerated from an obvious lack of understanding of American conditions, nor from the colonial attitude so apparent in their requests.

The two aspects of the German Catholic problem discussed here, while being fundamental, do not approach a thorough analysis of its eventual outcome. It would, perhaps, be quite interesting to bring in, for example, the ideal of total abstinence which the Irish Americanizers tried to enforce on the Germans who cherished their beer and continental observance of the Sunday; the pressures that were brought to bear on the appointment of English-speaking bishops each time an issue of succession arose in a German-populated diocese; Archbishop Ireland's far-sighted cooperation with the public school system in Faribault and Stillwater which caused

Germans, Jesuits, and conservatives among Catholics in the United States to call it an open attack on their cherished parochial school system; the conflict among Germans and Americanizers in the faculties of the Catholic University of America; the role of the first apostolic delegate to the United States, Francesco Cardinal Satoli, and his siding first with the liberals and then with the conservatives; the charges of Liberalism, Modernism and the lack of theological orthodoxy which were hurled at the Americanizers by German Catholic intellectuals; and finally, the events leading up to Pope Leo XIII's tempering encyclical letter on Americanism, *Testem Benevolentiae.*

The German Catholics eventually came to accept the position of the Americanizers, as did the other immigrant groups. Their mother tongue was dying out, American national habits were being assimilated, the United States was becoming recognized by them as a nation. No more protesting memorials were forwarded to Rome, since German parishes gradually became mixed parishes, national parishes slowly gave way to territorial parishes, and the German parishes became distinguished only by a spirit of German Catholicism as practiced by American citizens of German origin. Interest in the appointment of bishops of German ancestry and tongue became an academic question as the American Germans took their place in national life as one of the many elements that went to make up one people.

On the other hand, the Americanizers saw their program accomplished and their ideals fulfilled by this process of German assimilation. Their aims had unquestionably been progressive, but their means were sometimes questionable. The Americanizers on their part, ceased their intemperate charges about a conspiracy and came to realize in time the valuable contribution of Germans to life in the United States. The parochial school system, so vigorously defended by German Catholics, was accepted as a policy of the Church, several points of the Lucerne Memorial and the St. Raphael program, such as colonizing projects and care for immigrants and displaced persons were also incorporated into American Catholic practice. From the German examples of a strong press and vigorous society activity much was learned. The more spirited emphasis on use of the English language was left to time and environment rather than to stern admonitions which were open to misrepresentation and suspicion by immigrants not fully at home in American life. Perhaps, as more and more educators are now saying, the pluralistic linguistic and cultural values of the immigrant groups were recognized and respected too late in American life, and the values which individual nationality groups could contribute from their heritage to the enrichment of American life were not appreciated soon enough.

It is interesting today to watch growing demands for the teaching of foreign languages on all levels of the Catholic educational system. We have been going through a vigorous analysis of the quality of American Catholic intellectual life, and searching questions have been asked about our proportional contribution to cultural life and leadership. The record of German Catholic contributions has been limited, and a rewarding study could be made as to whether too hasty Americanization was a serious cause. Another area that awaits the historian of intellectual and religious life is the nature and character of American Catholic spirituality, or interior life, which has not been touched as yet. Why has there been a slow and reluctant response to the ideals of community worship, of the liturgical movement, of a respect for the Catholic traditions of participation, singing and a Scriptural-centered life? Were immigrant groups such as the Germans swept into the dominant current of the "American" secular cultural patterns? What happened to the ancient Catholic tradition of the arts and crafts in American Catholic life and educational institutions?

I personally think that such aspects of a Christian culture could have developed and received real impetus from immigrant groups like the Germans if they were not up-rooted and shorn of their true identity so rapidly and completely.

Apart from these considerations, the leaders of the Catholic Church in the United States who had encouraged Americanization made a contribution to the nation. Some nine million Catholic immigrants from over twenty countries had come to American shores in the century from 1820-1920. This vast number of settlers, almost half of the total net immigration to the United States of that period, was encouraged to understand and practice American democratic ideals by their new spiritual leaders. Divergent groups of people, like the Germans, were encouraged to amalgamate and adapt themselves. As a result a significant number of Catholic immigrants from Europe learned to live together as Americans.

Catholicism and Woman Suffrage

JAMES J. KENNEALLY

Politics has long furnished an important theatre for Catholic participation in American life—especially on the part of Irish Catholics—and there can be little doubt that it has functioned as a major means of adjustment and advancement for Catholics. Yet the criticism has often been made that Catholics backed politically conservative, if not disreputable, regimes and failed to lend their support to progressive candidates or reform programs. In the following article, James J. Kenneally, chairman of the history department at Stonehill College in North Easton, Massachusetts, examines one reform issue in detail in a single state. His investigation shows how intimately Catholic attitudes toward politics and reform were connected with a whole range of other issues: nativism, the school question, temperance, ethnic animosities, the development of the labor movement, fear of socialism, and the impact of war on social attitudes. The article indicates that Catholic lukewarmness toward reformers was not always based exclusively on ideological conservatism.

TRUE TO ITS TRADITION OF LEADERSHIP IN REFORM MOVEMENTS, the Commonwealth of Massachusetts played a vital role in the protracted struggle for women's political rights; not only were many feminist leaders born in the state but the first national women's rights convention was held there in Worcester in 1850. Yet this very agitation provoked strong forces of reaction which were able to delay the enfranchisement of Massachusetts women until 1920. Among these traditionalists were the Catholic clergy who desired not only to prevent a moral deterioration which suffrage could bring but who even feared the devel-

James J. Kenneally, "Catholicism and Woman Suffrage in Massachusetts," *Catholic Historical Review,* LIII (April, 1967), pp. 43-57. Reprinted without footnotes by permission of the author and the publisher.

opment of a political structure and social climate deleterious to Catholicism.

In 1885 when the Archbishop of Boston, John J. Williams, commented on the suffrage issue, he not only summarized the Catholic attitude to date but foreshadowed its position for the next thirty-five years. The Church does not involve itself in political questions; therefore it "leaves alone" the issue of woman suffrage; on the other hand, the archbishop cautioned, women should not take part in politics. The Catholic opposition to the participation of women in politics rested in the belief that there were two distinct spheres of activity, one for each sex. That of woman centered around her position in perpetuating the race and as nucleus of the society of the family. This was a system designed by God, revealed by a Pauline interpretation of scripture and/or the natural law, re-enforced by biological differences, and supported by a historical tradition which proclaimed the political supremacy of man. The usurpation by either sex of those activities which more properly belonged to the sphere of the other sex was unnatural, a threat to universal order. Since obviously women's voting was such a trespass, the Catholic press and clergy impressed upon the Catholic population of Massachusetts the dangerous consequences of encroaching upon these natural boundaries. The Bishop of Fall River, William Stang, not only feared that woman's position as "queen over the household" would be endangered by an interest in public affairs, but that even education would threaten it, because he pointed out, "smartness is not becoming women."

This Catholic fear for the safety of the home and motherhood was compounded a few years later by the juxtaposition of the birth-control movement with ballot extension. As married women could be active in politics only as a result of limiting their families, Margaret Sanger, founder of modern "planned parenthood," was convinced that female suffrage would lead to legal changes in those states which prohibited birth control. Consequently, she publicly endorsed the suffragist cause, while some suffragist leaders reciprocated by supporting Sanger's crusade. In 1915 the National Birth Control League was organized by women who were primarily active in the suffrage and feminist movements. The League's president, Mary Ware Dennett, was former field secretary of the Massachusetts Woman Suffrage Association and corresponding secretary of the National American Woman Suffrage Association, while one of its directors was Jessie Ashley, a former treasurer of the same group. An effective women's pressure group, the Massachusetts Association Opposed to the Further Extension of Suffrage to Women (frequently referred to as the MAOFESW), called public attention to the "sinister association" between these two groups. During the campaign of 1915, when the electorate was to vote on a constitutional amendment extending suffrage to women, this group distributed cards on election day depicting a woman wheeling her baby to the polls. The caption warned:

> The woman voter who has a child is handicapped by the necessity of pushing or carrying it to the polling place. Probably this is one of the reasons why so many suffragists favor the limitation of families, or what Col. Roosevelt calls "race suicide" and "professional motherhood" so that women might be "free" to exercise their equality with man.

The MAOFESW, charging that planned parenthood was being taught to young factory girls by socialists and suffragists, adopted a policy of encouraging "social purity" in order to check birth control. In addition to exposing the unseemly alliance the group was able to prevent the suffragists from conducting a birth control meeting in the Medford public library. Little wonder that some Catholics equated suffrage with birth control and that the first time Sanger was heckled at a public meeting was in Boston by a prominent convert to Catholicism and anti-suffragist, David Goldstein.

Catholic leaders not only warned their people against woman suffrage but also sought to influence the political process in order to prevent its extension. Among the signatories to the first male anti-woman suffrage petition submitted to the state legislature were John Boyle O'Reilly, editor of the Catholic newspaper, the Boston *Pilot,* and the Reverend Joshua P. Bodfish, chancellor of the Archdiocese of Boston. The following year, 1886, the opponents of woman suffrage brought their case directly to the General Court. An effective pamphlet was prepared, distributed to every member of the legislature, and circulated throughout the state; included in it were one of Bodfish's sermons and an appeal written by O'Reilly which although sardonic was much less caustic than his *Pilot* editorials. When both sexes were given the opportunity to express an opinion on the desirability of woman suffrage in the state elections of 1895 the Man Suffrage Association was established to obtain a "large no vote." Among its eminent supporters were Bodfish, Charles F. Donnelly, a prominent Catholic layman, friend and legal counselor to Archbishop Williams, and a young Congressman whose grandson would become president of the United States, John F. Fitzgerald. Meanwhile, the anti-suffrage tradition of the *Pilot* was assured when the novelist and poet James Jeffrey Roche succeeded O'Reilly as editor. Roche was in turn succeeded by Katherine Conway, who not only attacked suffrage in the *Pilot,* and in symposiums in the Boston *Globe, Donahoe's Magazine,* the *Catholic World* and in her book, *The Christian Gentlewoman and the Social Apostolate,* but was also active in the MAOFESW. A member of the Standing Committee of the Boston Branch, she protested against suffrage at a legislative hearing and worked with women members of the New England Press Association on behalf of that organization. Her activities in this cause, coupled with her position on the *Pilot,* were interpreted as far away as Baltimore as an indication of William Cardinal O'Connell's opposition to suffrage. Although O'Connell was opposed to suffrage, yet he never publicly and directly committed himself. On the other hand, through his attacks on feminism and a legislative protest by one of his intimate associates, his position was clear to astute observers.

One historian has stated that the opposition of the Massachusetts Catholic clergy was more intense than that of their colleagues throughout the nation, but it is apparent that their position accurately reflected American Catholic sentiment. The attacks on suffrage by James Cardinal Gibbons of Baltimore and Archbishops Henry Moeller of Cincinnati and Sebastian G. Messmer of Milwaukee seemed to reflect the sentiment of Catholic journals while the *Catholic Encyclopedia* not only described anti-suffrage groups as "the voice of common sense" but stated that "The female sex is in some respects inferior to the male sex as regards body and soul." The National American Woman Suffrage Association in 1900 was able to list but six Catholic clergymen in the nation who supported woman suffrage, while as late as 1915 the Church-Work Committee of that organization singled out as one of the suffragettes' most important tasks "the organization of the Catholic women, that they will make their demands so emphatic the church will see the wisdom of supporting the movement." Nevertheless, Lucy Burns was apparently the only nationally prominent Catholic suffrage leader.

The political activity of Massachusetts Catholic leadership to prevent suffrage was to a large extent understandable and justified. The Know-Nothing revival of the 1880's and 1890's directed a great deal of effort toward protecting the public schools from Catholic influence. The school committee franchise for women, enacted by the legislature in 1879, was used as a valuable weapon in this crusade and had the effect of associating woman suffrage and nativism in the Catholic mind.

In 1884 and 1885 a religious war fought with women's ballots was narrowly avoided; but the city was not so fortunate in 1888. In that year the Boston School Committee transferred a teacher for ridiculing Church doctrine on indulgences before his history class; furthermore, it dropped from its approved list the textbook which the teacher claimed substantiated his position. In July an angry group of nativists organized the Committee of One Hundred to protect the public schools from the Romanists; to aid in accomplishing this end it nominated its own slate for the school committee. This ticket was then endorsed by the Republican Party which had pledged at its state convention of 1887 to keep Massachusetts schools free from sectarian control. The British American Association, which had been established in 1887 to protect the state from Catholics, and its female counterpart, the Loyal Women of American Liberty, founded by an alleged ex-nun, quickly supported the objectives and candidates of the One Hundred. The political-religious turmoil so badly divided the Massachusetts School Suffrage Association (a political organization for better schools) that the Independent Women Voters, a nativist association, was formed from its membership. These women, along with the W.C.T.U., the other nativist groups, and a good many Boston ministers, exhorted women to register, vote, and save the public schools. Protestant women responded and the candidates of the Committee of One Hundred were swept into office on the strength of the largest feminine vote in Boston's history.

A few years later in Worcester, Massachusetts, a similar event occurred. The school committee of that city supported the Superintendent of Schools, Dr. A. P. Marble, against the accusation that he unduly favored Catholics in his hiring policy. But nativists with the aid of the women's ballot voted Marble's supporters off the school committee.

These incidents in which Protestant women voted and Catholic ones did not, convinced many nativists that a further extension of suffrage to women would be the means of protecting Massachusetts from Catholic contagion. This conviction was strengthened when the constant opposition of Catholic legislators to measures to extend suffrage to women was interpreted as a plot to "further the Romanists plans not to aid Protestant causes, or help on good movements." Consequently, in 1895 the Loyal Women, the Independent Women Voters, and the newly established American Protective Association urged the populace to vote "yes" on the desirability of extending municipal suffrage to women. Not only did they use the 1883 election as evidence of the value of woman suffrage but offered statistics to prove that even if foreign-born women exercised the franchise they would be out-voted by native-born women, an argument so wearisome that it offended the sensibilities of fair-minded citizens. Inevitably, Irish-Catholic men voted overwhelmingly against suffrage, while Irish-Catholic women hardly voted at all.

Even the respectable Massachusetts Woman Suffrage Association did not avoid the inclination to use suffrage as a means of defending Protestantism. Julia Ward Howe, one of the organization's founders and its first president, assailed Catholicism in her work *Modern Society,* while Mary A. Livermore, also a former president and sometime editor of the organization's newspaper, the *Woman's Journal,* hailed the results of the 1888 election as cleansing the school committee "of the sectarian Catholic influence, that had begun an injurious domination of the public schools." Furthermore, the co-operation of the organization with nativists for suffrage increased Catholic suspicion of the Association and its cause. One of Boston's leading anti-Catholic clergymen, Joseph Cook, addressed its annual meeting in 1892 and was the principal suffrage speaker at legislative hearings in 1891. Eliza Trask Hill, the president of the Independent Women Voters, testified for suffrage in the hearings of 1892, 1893, and 1895, while the 1893 legislative petition for woman suffrage was a joint presentation of the Massachusetts Woman Suffrage Association, the Loyal Women of American Liberty, and the Independent Women Voters. The *Woman's Journal*—although non-committal on the religious issues of 1884, 1885, and 1888—welcomed the turmoil, believing that anything which led to a larger woman's vote was desirable. Even more inflammatory to Catholics was the attack on the venerable Senator George F. Hoar, a long-time suffragist, before the largest suffrage rally during the campaign of 1895, due to his defense of Catholic rights against the assertions of the A.P.A. In addition, the chairman of the meeting reproved those women who hired Catholics as domestics. As Thomas Wentworth Higginson observed, many women had come to view the ballot as a means of repressing the Catholic Church. By 1902, when the Massachusetts Woman Suffrage Association attempted to establish a special committee to work among Catholics, it could not find Catholic women with the necessary leisure or inclination to serve on it.

Despite the fact that hints of anti-Catholicism lingered on into the twentieth-century suffrage movement, Catholic sentiment slowly began to change. As early as 1888, emotions had become so aroused that from 6,000 to 7,000 Catholic women ignored the archbishop's non-involvement plea and voted in the election for school committee, while other Catholics anticipated a possible future need to marshal a force of Catholic women voters to protect "true Americanism and Christianity." Then in what was described as the "greatest individual accession" to suffrage ranks in the year 1895, the Reverend Thomas Scully, the prominent pastor of St. Mary's in Cambridge, became the first Massachusetts priest to support publicly the extension of suffrage to women. Scully, the director of the Catholic Total Abstinence Union of Boston, was first attracted to the cause when he supported liquor-license suffrage for women in 1889. As he believed it "unjust to allow men who are inferior to women in all moral, educational, and social matters to vote, and deny that right to women," he soon embraced the entire movement. In 1896 he addressed the state woman suffrage convention and in 1897 and 1899 defended suffrage before legislative committees.

Even more significant than Scully's support were the changes in the state itself. The election of the first Catholic to state-wide office, David I. Walsh to the Lieutenant-Governorship in 1912, was indicative of a decline in anti-Catholic nativism, thus making possible a Catholic judgment of suffrage purely on its merits. Meanwhile Massachusetts labor, swelled by an influx of female members, intensified its suffrage commitment to such an extent that by 1911 it had become one of labor's major objectives. Large numbers of Catholic union members began to see suffrage as a means of improving working conditions, and Catholics witnessed labor leaders such as John F. Tobin, President of the Boot and Shoe Workers Union, and Michael A. Murphy of the Central Labor Union, testify before the legislature for suffrage. Mary K. O'Sullivan personified these changing attitudes. After organizing the bindery workers in Boston into the Ladies Federal Union, she became an organizer for the AFL and one of the founders of the National Women's Trade Union, established in Faneuil Hall, Boston. Representing the trade unions at the legislative hearings on woman suffrage in 1908, she accused representatives of the MAOFESW:

> Not one of you have ever raised your voice in the interest of women wage earners. You do not know how or probably care how the women live who make your shoes or clothes. To me women who oppose this measure are enemies of the people. . . . Mr. Chairman, these women are in the same category as those who take the place of strikers.

As Catholics throughout the nation became more responsive toward the suffrage cause, it became necessary for churchmen to clarify opposition to suffrage which had commonly been misinterpreted as official teaching rather than individual opinion. Not only was the Church's position clarified but Austin Dowling, Bishop of Des Moines, joined the suffrage ranks while Cardinal Gibbons despite his forebodings admitted the inevitable victory of the women's cause. One anti-suffrage publication even believed it necessary to assure Catholics that theologically the suffrage question was still "open" and that they were free to oppose it. In Boston, Cardinal O'Connell, who had once promised to attack woman suffrage publicly if necessary to prevent its extension, now changed his mind and refused to take a public stand. Instead, the Boston *Pilot,* which he had recently purchased, criticized women's groups for trying to get the Church involved in a question which it described as a political issue. In keeping with his policy, the chancery office rebuffed the MAOFESW when it requested co-operation in presenting its message to Catholic women's clubs and refused to express an opinion on a circular "Catholics on Suffrage."

Nevertheless, the Cardinal's sentiments on suffrage were implied in his frequent sallies against feminism; one of his speeches on the subject was reprinted and distributed by the National Association Opposed to Woman Suffrage. Even his attacks on socialism had some anti-suffrage overtones. In 1910 a series of anti-socialist meetings was conducted under his auspices the fourth of which—whose subject was the family—was conducted by the diocesan chancellor, Monsignor Michael J. Splaine. He stated that woman's place was the home, where she should preside as queen and source of inspiration. Two prominent converts to Catholicism,

David Goldstein and Martha Moore Avery, were more adamant. Life-long friends and socialists before their conversion, they linked frequently in their writings the extension of suffrage to a "Red menace," observing that the socialist movement had long supported the woman's cause. Avery debated woman suffrage with the President of the National American Woman Suffrage Association, Dr. Anna H. Shaw, at Faneuil Hall; she also attacked it at the legislative hearings of 1908, 1910, 1914, and 1915. In 1919 during the "Red Scare," Goldstein, by then a noted lecturer on socialism, was the featured speaker at a Tremont Temple meeting organized and conducted under the MAOFESW and directed against "Socialism, Bolshevism and Woman Suffrage." Before 2,500 persons, he denounced socialism for endangering the home, and related it to woman suffrage, which he condemned as destructive of the moral influence of women. Less than a year later in Baltimore, he addressed the State Defense League, an organization of men who defended states rights against a federal suffrage amendment. In a speech entitled "The Dangers of Radicalism" he repeated his canard that suffrage and socialism were inseparable.

O'Connell's private hostility and public neutrality to suffrage were probably typical of the attitude of the Massachusetts clergy. Nevertheless, Catholics became more active in the movement. By 1913 Mrs. Teresea A. Crowley was legislative agent of the Massachusetts Woman Suffrage Association and chairman of the Good Government Board of the Boston Equal Suffrage League. Much more dramatic were the activities of Margaret Foley. In 1911, followed by a group of women, she shadowed the Republican candidate for governor, Louis A. Frothingham, an anti-suffragist, on his campaign in the western part of the state, interrupting his rallies, heckling his speeches, haranguing his followers, and contributing substantially toward his defeat. She successfully repeated these tactics in 1913 when the President of the Masssachusetts Senate, Levi Greenwood, packed the Committee on Constitutional Amendments against the suffragists. She distributed anti-Greenwood literature at his rallies; lectured to his crowds, and handed out over 30,000 circulars in the factories there. Even Greenwood acknowledged these activities as the major cause of his defeat.

Catholic suffragettes also supported their favorites. In 1914 when Walsh, sympathetic to suffrage, ran for re-election as governor, they shared the platform with him at his rallies and spoke for their own cause. When the legislature passed a suffrage amendment to the state constitution at Walsh's request, the question was submitted to the voters for ratification. During the summer and fall of 1915, as Walsh campaigned for his third term, he not only endorsed ratification but tried unsuccessfully to get a suffrage plank in the Democratic platform and linked his re-election bid with the woman's cause. The close rapport between Catholicism and suffrage, significantly attained since 1888, was further reflected in the support of the suffrage amendment by the Catholic Order of Foresters, and the Catholic Democratic paper the *Republic,* as well as by an absence of attacks by the clergy and Catholic press. Despite shifting Catholic sentiment both the amendment and Walsh lost. But Walsh's large vote and suffrage conviction, in the face of a re-united Republican Party, encouraged suffragettes to view him as one of their champions. In 1918, when he campaigned for the senate seat of John W. Weeks, a dedicated opponent of a federal suffrage amendment, suffragettes campaigned vigorously for Walsh; among other activities a nonpartisan committee of Catholic women worked among their coreligionists on his behalf. These activities were among the major factors to which Weeks attributed his defeat.

Meanwhile, Catholic women, like those in New York and Philadelphia, organized their own state-wide suffrage association with the aid of Margaret Foley. The Margaret Brent Suffrage Guild under the presidency of Mrs. Evelyn H. Scanlan, a former school-teacher, dedicated itself to full suffrage for women. Although the organization was coldly received by O'Connell who neither spoke before it nor appointed a spiritual director to it, it had large public meetings with guest speakers and sent representatives to legislative hearings. O'Connell must have been further dismayed when the President of the League of Catholic Women, a group organized under his guidance and of which he was honorary president, journeyed to Baltimore with other Catholic suffragettes in an effort to convince Cardinal Gibbons to end his attacks on suffrage.

Despite the reservations of many of the clergy, some priests began to support the movement; one of the most noteworthy was a self-described feminist, the Reverend Jones Corrigan, S.J., chairman of the Department of Philosophy at Boston College. In an address before an audience of over 500 at Boston's Hotel Westminster, Corrigan rhetorically asked, "Who better could stand on the platform for suffrage than a Catholic priest?"

A rather unusual question, for his textbook on special ethics which had been used at Boston College as recently as four years before, condemned the political rights of women as contrary to the natural law. This radical shift in view was due in part to the fact that Corrigan was an effective popularizer of current ideas rather than an original scholar. The contributions of women to the war effort, which had become an effective and popular argument for entitling women to vote, was one of the major justifications presented by Corrigan. Furthermore, he asserted that suffrage should be extended because in a democracy women had a moral right to vote; even more important, with forty out of every hundred females of voting age in the state engaged in industry, the ballot was necessary for the improvement of working conditions. On the other hand, he warned suffragettes against entangling alliances with radicals who hoped to use the movement for easy divorce, free love, and birth control, which would divert the true purpose of the reform, "better and cleaner social welfare." Corrigan concluded his address by expressing hope that Massachusetts would be among the first states to ratify the federal amendment.

His hope was soon realized. The legislature, many members of which were now convinced that women's war work entitled them to the ballot, overwhelmingly ratified the Nineteenth Amendment. Fourteen months later the thirty-sixth state, Tennessee, also ratified the amendment, which now became law. Clerical spokesmen in Massachusetts remained silent on this momentous change. But they probably believed, like those Catholics who expressed a view, that voting was now a duty which Catholic women should exercise with wisdom and prudence. Thus the Catholic leadership of Massachusetts who had reluctantly abandoned oposition to woman suffrage as a result of changing social conditions and lay attitudes had come full cycle and demonstrated Catholic assimilation of American values. The "dubious" reform was accepted in accordance with the political heritage and with an optimistic hope, not too unlike that of American humanistic tradition, for a better society.

Pro-Germanism and American Catholicism, 1914-1917

EDWARD CUDDY

The "Americanization" movement and campaign against "hyphenation" of the World War I era presented new challenges of adjustment to American Catholics. An immigrant people with ties to several of the warring powers in Europe, Catholics were torn by conflicting sympathies. Many of them disapproved of the policy followed by the Wilson Administration, yet they were keenly sensitive to the charge of being less than fully loyal to the United States. A recent work, Dorothy Dohen's *Nationalism and American Catholicism* (1967), argues that Catholics have historically overcompensated for their social insecurity with a chauvinistic superpatriotism; yet during the years 1914-1917 Catholics were suspected of divided loyalties and pro-Germanism. Professor Edward Cuddy of Rosary Hill College in Buffalo examines the pro-Germanism charge, showing the diversity of Catholic reactions to the war and linking those reactions to the themes of ethnicity and Americanization.

WHEN EUROPE WENT TO WAR IN AUGUST, 1914, ONE BASIC sentiment dominated the American public: the preservation of peace on this side of the Atlantic. President Wilson's plea for impartiality in thought, however, had little more than rhetorical appeal for the American people. The nation's strong Anglo-Saxon tradition and its long-standing friendship for France oriented public opinion toward the

Edward Cuddy, "Pro-Germanism and American Catholicism, 1914-1917," *Catholic Historical Review*, LIV (October, 1968), pp. 427-429, 437-442, 444-447, 450-454. Reprinted without footnotes and with deletions by permission of the author and the publisher.

Allies. But America's polyglot population, with ethnic ties to most of the warring countries, made her vulnerable to propaganda favoring both sets of belligerents.

As the war progressed, a vigorous coalition of Irish- and German-Americans worked diligently to counteract pro-Ally influences in American life and diplomacy. The Catholic Church in America adopted a policy of official neutrality toward the war. But some strands of evidence suggest that powerful Irish and German influences within American Catholicism oriented it toward the Central Powers. England had a good many enemies in the United States, complained the British ambassador, "and the Irish have lent their unequalled power of political organization to Jews, Catholics and Germans." With one or two exceptions, declared one pro-German Irishman, the many Catholic papers "waste few words in favor of the British government in this war." Historians in recent years have also suggested that Catholic influence favored the Central Powers, but no one has expressed a stronger statement than that of Arthur S. Link. "Reflecting its predominantly Irish- and German-American constituency and the Vatican's friendship for the Hapsburg dynasty," declares Professor Link, "the Roman Catholic Church in the United States—hierarchy, priesthood, and press—tended toward an open partisanship." Link ventured this opinion in the absence of any systematic survey of Catholic opinion during the war. This essay, developed from an intensive examination of the alleged pro-Germanism within the Church, may contribute to a broader understanding of the complex Catholic response to the European conflict prior to American entry into the war.

Catholicism during the Wilson era was a many-splendored thing. A rich diversity of ethnic stocks, a variety of internal and external pressures, and a plethora of organs expressing Catholic sentiment produced a diversified response to the conflict that had suddenly erupted across the Atlantic. The sheer variety of Catholic wartime attitudes makes generalizations about the Church extremely difficult. In general, two basic themes dominated Catholic opinion during the period of neutrality: the preservation of American neutrality and the restoration of peace to Europe. . . .

Behind the façade of official neutrality, however, Catholics like most other Americans fell far short of President Wilson's ideal, to be "impartial in thought as well as in action." Irish and German elements did affect the Church's stance toward the European conflict; but so did other ethnic groups as well as the pro-Ally influences that played upon the entire American population. Hence, there was a spectrum of opinion within the American Church which ranged from the strong pro-German sympathies of the German Catholic press to the consistently pro-Ally commentary appearing in the *Catholic World*. In analyzing the Church's response to the belligerents, then, diversity rather than uniformity is the phenomenon we must examine.

• • •

The diversity of Catholic wartime opinion is aptly illustrated by the many faces of Woodrow Wilson which appeared in the Catholic press during those trying years. Reports during the submarine crisis ranged from the *Tablet's* exuberant claim that "Catholic America is with the President," to *Die Amerika's* conclusion that Wilson had become "the lackey of the King of England." After the president launched his military preparedness program in December, 1915, he found himself again in the crossfire of a divided American opinion. His program, too little, too late, according to militarists, bore the seeds of war according to pacifists. And Catholic opinion fell on both sides of the ledger.

The presidential campaign of 1916 indicated further the cleavage in Catholic opinion over Wilsonian leadership. For nearly two years, the president's Mexican policy had provoked sharp criticism in the diocesan press while his European policy was alienating the pro-German element in the Church. Unfortunately, tensions stimulated by the war boiled over into the bitter "anti-hyphen" campaign in which Wilson's role widened considerably the circle of Catholic disenchantment. As Irish- and German-American leaders continued their assault on Wilson's neutrality policies, the president lashed back at his "hyphenated" critics whose loyalty to their European homelands, he felt, prejudiced their American patriotism. The current attack on hyphenism reflected a legitimate concern over the divisive loyalties of an immigrant nation and enjoyed substantial support from the American public. But the episode grated on Catholic sensibilities, for it smacked of the anti-Catholic, anti-immigrant strains in the American nativist tradition. . . .

By election time the Catholic vote was quivering to tremors created by war in Europe and revolution in Mexico. Several factors, however, prevented a Catholic stampede from the Democratic Party. Ethnic feeling varied greatly throughout the Church, and many Catholics repudiated the rabid pro-Germanism of those who had turned against the president. A Catholic anti-Wilson vote, as more responsible leaders perceived, would only reinforce current charges that the Church was trying to take over the government. The Administration's pro-labor policies reinforced the Democratic tendencies of the Catholic working class. And Wilson's valiant efforts to preserve the peace were not lost on the Catholic electorate. "Fortunately, we have a government today," declared Archbishop John Glennon, of St. Louis, "which refuses to be influenced by the Jingo and the chauvinist at home, or lured by those abroad to a war for increasing empire or world domination." In retrospect, neither ethnic antagonism stirred by the war nor resentment over Mexico seems to have converted Catholic loyalties into a Republican vote.

With the campaign behind him, President Wilson resumed the task, pursued intermittently since January, 1915, of bringing the belligerents to the conference table. But Germany stole the initiative in December by declaring her readiness to discuss peace terms. Wilson responded with notes to both sets of belligerents asking them to state their objectives. Catholic supporters of the Reich naturally interpreted the initial peace proposal as fresh evidence of Germany's honorable intentions in the war. But the prospect of peace restored to war-torn Europe stirred a broad segment of the Catholic community. Some spokesmen were especially impressed by Germany's apparent effort to include the Vatican in her peace plans. By transmitting her peace note to Rome, *America* observed, the imperial government "officially recognized" the pope as the "supreme defender of the cause of peace." Unfortunately, this eleventh-hour quest for peace faltered amidst the wartime hatreds and national ambitions of the belligerent powers. The peace effort collapsed, according to pro-German Catholics, because the Allies had rejected Germany's "Generous and Noble Proposal to Save Further Bloodshed."

On January 31, 1917, Germany announced her decision to resume unrestricted submarine warfare; and Washington replied by severing diplomatic relations three days later. As American opinion drifted slowly toward war, the profound peace sentiment within the Church resisted the current. The Church's leaders called for calm and patience during the crisis. The inflammatory Zimmermann note and the shocking destruction of American ships in mid-March were scarcely noticed by the Catholic press. Some pro-Germans defended Germany's actions, reaffirmed the

American isolationist tradition, and denounced both the one-sidedness of American diplomacy and the war spirit fostered by profit-hungry munitions makers. Even as Germany's most provocative actions were pushing this nation toward war, the Indiana *Catholic* hummed with criticism of British oppression in Ireland and pro-war Anglo-Saxon influences in America.

But peace, even in Catholic circles, was not an absolute. As American neutrality withered away, ecclesiastical spokesmen seemed to work overtime to maintain a united front among their immigrant constituency. Many will be tested, observed one editor, because of the lands from which they came. But unity was essential, he insisted, and "it is only for us to follow as our leaders proclaim." Though Ireland inspire "our hate [*sic*] of England," declared one Irish Catholic orator, "that hate must express itself in a deeper and more ardent love for America and for what she stands."

When Congress finally declared war on April 6 [1917], some German Catholics were still bitter over the turn of events which now pitted their adopted land against their fatherland. But the call of Cardinal William O'Connell, Archbishop of Boston, for "absolute unity" in support of the national war effort expressed the prevailing mood in American Catholicism. "There is no government in the world today more entitled to the loyalty and devotion of its Catholic citizens," declared Bishop John P. Farrelly, of Cleveland, "than is that of the United States. . . ." Other members of the hierarchy shared these convictions as they proceeded to mobilize the faithful in support of the war effort.

The German High Command undoubtedly played the major role in transforming Catholic peace sentiment into wartime patriotism. But other factors contributed significantly to this transition. America's struggle, according to Wilsonian rhetoric, was for the universal right of all nations to self-determination. To many Irish Catholics the president's words linked American victory to Irish freedom and thereby eased their acceptance of Great Britain as a wartime partner. America's role in the war, the Irish press insisted, committed her to Ireland's freedom "on the distinct and unequivocal statement by the president that America's object is the promotion of Democracy and the restoration of their rights to all the oppressed peoples of Europe."

In addition, a peculiar strain of self-conscious patriotism conditioned the Catholic response to the crisis. For a people badgered by repeated charges of "divided loyalty," war offered a rare opportunity to demonstrate their genuine Americanism. In the summer of 1917 the Knights of Columbus Commission on Religious Prejudices triumphantly reported that Catholics led the way in meeting the present crisis. "Here is an answer to the bigots' erstwhile cry of disloyalty," the report continued, "one more powerful than words." Catholics, "responsive to the teaching and traditions of their Church," were proving "that it is noble to serve and holy to die for one's country." Widespread was the hope that the wartime exhibition of Catholic patriotism would silence the Church's critics and guarantee her status as a full-fledged American institution.

The most difficult task of this study has been the formulation of adequate generalizations which sum up the Catholic response to the issues of neutrality. Despite official declarations of peace and neutrality, the Catholic press refracted into a broad spectrum of varying sympathies for the European belligerents. And the question remains whether or not ethnic influences prompted the Church to "lean" toward Germany and her Allies. The answer to this question, hedged with difficulties, can appeal only to those sympathetic with the limits of historical generalization.

. . . [A] case can be made for the position that the Catholic press inclined toward the Kaiser. A thriving German Catholic press, supplemented by a few papers edited by Irish zealots, yielded a spectrum of press opinion more heavily pro-German than pro-Ally.* Moreover, many neutral Catholics, distressed over the munitions trade, inclined toward a moderate American submarine policy, and anxious to preserve the peace, helped to reinforce the pro-German position. . . .

These considerations, however, fall short of proving that the American Church abandoned neutrality to support the German cause. . . .

The pro-German papers . . . were particularly subject to strong ethnic influences and generally limited to areas with heavy German populations. Catholic periodicals with a national circulation like *America, Extension,* and *Our Sunday Visitor* were basically non-partisan while one of the oldest and best known journals, the *Catholic World,* supported the Allies.

* At this point, Professor Cuddy's original article provides a table showing seven Catholic publications as "Pro-German"; five as "Neutral but with muted sympathy for Germany"; nine as "Genuinely Neutral"; two as "Neutral but with muted sympathy for the Allies"; and one as "Pro-Ally." [Editor's note]

The most distinguished diocesan papers like the Boston *Pilot* and the Brooklyn *Tablet* tried to hold to a strictly neutral line.

Finally, if the Catholic press embraced the German cause, it was certainly lost on many German-Americans. There were "few Catholic American papers," noted one German-American editor, "that can be truly said to adhere to a strictly neutral attitude in the present war." . . . Father William Engelen, S.J., provoked at anti-German attitudes in some Catholic publications, considered a *Catholic World* article a prime example of "stupidity, malice, insinuation, distortion, half-truth, abuse and misrepresentation."

The Catholic press, therefore, was bitterly denounced for its anti-German tendencies and scored by later historians for its pro-German tendencies. This paradoxical phenomenon reinforces our conviction that Catholic journalism, marked by a wide diversity of opinion, generally occupied the broad middle ground of neutrality during the Wilson era.

• • •

In assessing the Catholic reaction to the European conflict, historians have neglected potent sociological factors which braked an ethnic-based pro-Germanism within church walls. For decades, Catholic leaders had struggled to preserve a fragile unity within their multi-ethnic constituency and to integrate their immigrant Church into the larger American society. The pursuit of these two historic objectives imposed firm restraints on immigrant nationalism. A generation before the war broke out, these issues were fought out in a bitter struggle by some German Catholics to structure the Church along ethnic lines. To Irish-American bishops like Gibbons and John Ireland, this so-called Cahensly movement threatened both the internal unity of the Church and the prompt Americanization of the immigrant while exposing ecclesiastical affairs to foreign political influence. Backed by Leo XIII, the "Americanizers" succeeded in suppressing the movement. In a sense, the issues joined in the Cahensly controversy were revived by the European conflict. Open support for either belligerent posed an obvious threat to the fragile bonds that held together the Church's immigrant groups. Father Peter Dietz felt obliged to curb his sympathies for the fatherland because, as he put it, "I represent the Catholic Societies, made up of the various nationalities, now engaged in the conflict." Should the Central Verein succumb to "nationalistic tendencies," Frederick Kenkel feared, its religious influence would be undermined. Responsible journalists wrote with the conviction that "it is not the province of a strictly Catholic paper, representing peoples of many races, to be partisan. . . ."

The Church's relentless effort to overcome its immigrant status also became a potent deterrent to pro-Germanism within its confines. "You can't be Germans or descendants of Germans in the United States," declared Bishop Peter J. Muldoon, of Rockford, to the German Catholic Union of Illinois, "you must be Americans. The Germans, the Irish, the Italians, the French, the Bohemians, and all others, must forget that they are anything but children of God, and must work for God and their country, America. Good Catholics," he insisted, "are good Americans." The theme was forcefully restated in papers like the *Catholic Union and Times,* which reminded its readers that their country was "not Germany, or Poland, or France, or Belgium, or Italy, or Austria, or even Ireland— it is the United States of America.". . .

An upsurge of religious bigotry which continued into the early years of the war lent additional impetus to Catholic efforts to gain acceptance in American society. In an atmosphere where Catholics were suspect of "divided loyalties," Catholic leaders redoubled their efforts to prove that neither devotion to the Papacy nor ties to the European homeland hindered a Catholic allegiance to the United States. Innumerable press reports on the heroism of Catholics serving in the German, Austrian, French, and English armies drew the moral that the faithful the world over were inspired by their religion to fight and die for their own country. This theme was explored in Guilday's syndicated column on "Hero Priests" in the war, written at the request of his ordinary, the Archbishop of Philadelphia, in the hope of "allaying somewhat the anti-Catholic campaign we have been suffering under, here in the East." Catholic soldiers continued to fight despite Vatican appeals for peace. And this fact, gloated one paper, refuted current charges that Catholic political loyalties were determined by "blind obedience 'to the dictation of the Pope of Rome. . . .'"

Religious considerations notwithstanding, ethnic loyalties in certain quarters worked against the Church's neutrality in the war. But the "Americanization of Catholicism," as a continuing process, deflected the thrust of nationalistic forces within the Church.

A third factor, the international character of Catholicism, also buttressed ecclesiastical neutrality toward belligerent powers. The tragedy of an embattled Europe was also the tragedy of a divided Catholicism. And a moral affinity with the faithful on both sides of the firing line undoubtedly dampened partisan attitudes springing from ethnic loyalties. . . .

In summary, pro-German tendencies within the Church sprang from an immigrant nationalism which rubbed abrasively against the cosmopolitan character of Catholicism. The historic objectives of the Church in this country as well as the unity of the Church universal were better served by three wartime themes: peace, neutrality, and patriotism. And these themes rather than partisanship for either belligerent dominated the complex Catholic response toward the European conflict.

At certain times and in certain places, neutrality wore thin. And the spectrum of expressed Catholic opinion, which weighed more heavily in favor of the Central Powers than toward the Allies, gives some substance to the observation that the Church "leaned" toward the former. Still, there remained a sharp cleavage between the mainstream of Catholic journalism and the pro-German line in this country—sharp enough to arouse suspicions in German-America that Catholic spokesmen had betrayed them. With some reservations, we conclude that American Catholicism, in the main, remained faithful to the official American policy of neutrality.

Catholic opinion, as such, exercised little or no direct influence on American diplomacy during the perplexing years, 1914-1917. But the Church's indirect social influence must not be overlooked. Her strong insistence on peace, amid jingoistic outbursts, broadened support for Wilson's peace policy. The Church's persistent effort to unite her immigrant children helped to cement a polyglot nation pulled by conflicting loyalties. And her emphatic demands for loyalty to the United States and obedience to her leaders helped dispose millions of Americans for the painful enterprise of war when it finally came in April, 1917.

Catholicism and Americanism in the 1930s

DAVID J. O'BRIEN

After the controversies of the 1880s and 1890s, American Catholicism entered on a period marked by numerical growth and absorption in internal institutional development. Especially after the papal condemnation of Modernism in 1907, the American Catholic scene became ideologically quiescent and intellectually stagnant. Only in the area of social reform was there a continuation of anything that could be called Catholic liberalism. Activities in this area, however, were usually carried on with only superficial attention to the theoretical problems involved in the interaction of Catholicism and the American tradition. In the most recent period interest in these problems has increased markedly; an outstanding study which examines earlier social reform activities with a sophisticated awareness of the theoretical dimension is David J. O'Brien's *American Catholics and Social Reform: The New Deal Years* (1968). The conclusion to that book, reproduced below, reveals something of the diversity of Catholic social movements in the 1930s and of how they are evaluated by a scholar representative of a later generation of Catholic liberalism. Mr. O'Brien is Associate Professor of History at the College of the Holy Cross, Worcester, Massachusetts.

IN THE 1930'S A REMARKABLE NUMBER OF CATHOLICS DEVOTED THEIR attention to social and economic problems. The publication of *Quadragesimo Anno* in 1931 provided an authoritative basis for analysis and action, but it was the Depression that caught the attention of Church leaders and made the entire Catholic community more receptive to papal teachings than ever before. Nevertheless, in the United States as elsewhere, acceptance of papal authority did not imply uniformity of opinion on concrete issues. Instead Catholic social thought in the 1930's was characterized by unanimous and enthusiastic approval of official Church teachings and wide, often bitter, disagreement over their meaning and application. This troubled many American Catholics who believed that the Church possessed a distinctive goal and method for reform offering cures for all the nation's ills, a conviction strengthened by Pius XI's prescriptions for Christian social reconstruction. Few thought that the Church possessed no such model of society as it ought to be, that its "answers" could not be translated into solutions for pressing national problems. Yet the necessarily indefinite character of the Church's positive teachings was revealed in the decade by the inability of reform-minded Catholics to agree on the merits of secular programs, or formulate their own alternatives, and in the alacrity with which many responded to a negative anti-communism which possessed the clear and authoritative sanction the reformers lacked.

Some of the most heated controversy centered around the question of federal jurisdiction in national life. In 1932 almost all Catholic spokesmen agreed that the severity of the Depression, the collapse of private charities, and the weakness of state and local authorities necessitated federal intervention. This position represented a sharp break for American Catholics, long accustomed to viewing constitutional limitations on the national government as protective bulwarks against potential anti-Catholic persecution. Those Catholics who were most conscious of the Church's minority status warned that emergency grants of power were temporary and should be rescinded when the crisis had passed. As the pressures of unemployment did subside, such warnings became more frequent until, by 1937, concern over the growth of the federal government was nearly universal among articulate Catholic leaders.

Fear of latent anti-Catholicism was only one reason for such constitutional scruples. American Catholicism had responded to the needs of its immigrant population by constructing an enormous network of schools, hospitals, orphanages, and other benevolent institutions whose existence dictated a policy of caution in dealing with public assistance. William

F. Montavon stated this position clearly in his 1933 report of the NCWC*
administrative board. "The welfare of religion is closely tied up with the
problem of federalism," he wrote. "Because of divergent and conflicting
views, the larger the scope of any political authority in our country, the
more rigidly must it adhere to a policy of minimum interference in controversial matters." At first glance this fact appeared congenial to a religious minority, but Montavon pointed out that it meant, in religious
terms, "secularism." "Local authorities," on the other hand, covered a
smaller area and were often able to "do things a federal agency could not
do," a fact which directly affected "schools, benevolent agencies," and
charities. The implication was clear. As long as relief, education, and aid
to charitable endeavors were left in local hands, urban Catholic majorities
might be translated, if not into direct assistance to private agencies, at least
into a benevolent neutrality that would protect them against secular competitors armed with public funds. The interests of the institutional Church
thus blended with the fears of the Catholic minority to shape a political
outlook hostile to the permanent extension of national power.

This view could find support in papal teachings, but appeals to Church
authority posed serious problems. The corporate assumptions of papal
social teachings challenged the individualism of American society, the
freedom of economic enterprise, and the decentralized structure of American political institutions. The goals and methods of Catholic social action,
as outlined in *Quadragesimo Anno,* involved a basic confrontation of the
Catholic with his society. Total commitment could well awaken latent
anti-Catholicism and revive charges of Catholic disloyalty to American
values. More important, such a confrontation would precipitate a crisis
for Catholics themselves, for they had long ago accepted as their own
many of the principles and practices which Catholic teachings called into
question.

The result was that Catholics invariably sought to justify their position
by reference not only to Church authorities but to American traditions as
well, asserting the compatibility, even the identity, of "true Americanism" and orthodox Catholicism. This assertion had always been a central
theme of the American Catholic mind. Since the days when Bishop Car-

---

* NCWC is the abbreviation for National Catholic Welfare Conference. The
national organization of the American bishops, now known as the United States
Catholic Conference, was established in 1919. [Editor's note]

roll organized the American Church, Catholics had never ceased telling Rome and native Protestants that Catholic religious teachings and American political and social beliefs complemented each other perfectly. "To understand the Catholic Church in America," wrote the Church's leading historian in 1926, "one must see how naturally and integrally the spiritual allegiance of its members knits into the national allegiance so as to round each other out." This argument of course required some definition of "true Americanism." Often it seemed merely to denote a consensus on individual natural rights and governmental responsibility for social justice. More frequently it meant a specific assertion that the philosophy of American government was similar to that of traditional Catholic political philosophy. Historical proof could be found in the work of Catholic scholars who demonstrated the influence of the political thought of Robert Bellarmine on the writings of Thomas Jefferson on the Declaration of Independence, thus providing an historical basis for the argument that America was "Catholic in philosophical principle." The corollary was that, contrary to the slanders of fundamentalist Protestants and secular liberals, the nation had no more ardent or sincere defenders than her Catholic citizens.

Yet in much of the popular writing such arguments were implied and the conclusions assumed, so that professions of loyalty to America and assertions of compatibility of American and Catholic values took the place of detailed argumentation. In either case "Americanism" remained a vague body of values subject to varying interpretations and emphasis; the ideals of the Declaration of Independence and the structure of the Constitution have always been subject to such varying interpretations by all Americans. Catholics were within the American consensus described by so many recent historians, but its acceptance only provided a framework for the discussion of political and social issues; it did not eliminate conflict, or make conflict insignificant. Like Christianity it could provide sanctions for laissez-faire *and* social justice, decentralization *and* federal action, individual rights and liberties *and* the general welfare and the common good. The fact that the balance of these polarities was not struck once and for all by either an authoritative American institution or by the Papacy meant that both "Americanism" and Catholicism easily became sources of support, of emotionally charged symbols to provide a sanction for positions that originated in economic and social conditions.

American Catholics wanted to believe that being a Catholic and being an American both had clear, unambiguous meaning—the same meaning—so that they used the terms as if they had that meaning. In so doing, they missed the point that neither was subject to final formulation, at least in political and social terms.

Professions of loyalty to fundamental American values were common in American Catholic history. In the late nineteenth century John Ireland and his followers enthusiastically defended their country against its European detractors. They deplored Catholic separatism and aloofness and urged a policy of Americanization which would simultaneously make the Church a more effective force in society and reform the Church in the spirit of American democracy. More recently this attitude has reawakened with far greater force, expressing itself in a ferment of criticism of Catholic intellectual life, liturgical practice, and Church organization and in a drive to end once and for all the internal preoccupations, moral self-righteousness, and social irresponsibility of "ghetto Catholicism." This emphasis upon assimilation and adaptation depends upon an assumption that the American environment contains nothing that fundamentally conflicts with the principles of Christianity. For liberal Catholics of the 1890's and 1950's this seemed obvious, but it was otherwise for Catholics in the interwar years. In the twenties the strength of anti-Catholicism together with the aftereffects of the condemnations of modernism and Americanism weakened attempts to maintain the liberal policies of Ireland and Cardinal Gibbons and stifled the zeal for reform emanating from the Social Action Department. Yet, while adopting a stance of militant defensiveness, Catholic leaders by no means rejected America. On the contrary they argued that the nativism, materialism, and secularism of the period were untrue to the authentic spirit of American life. Far from denouncing the cry of Americanism so often used by anti-Catholic spokesmen, Catholics adopted it, arguing that, as Father James Gillis wrote after the defeat of Al Smith, "We found ourselves more in harmony with true Americanism than they were who denied our right to be American."

In the 1930's the situation changed. Fundamentalist Protestants no longer posed a serious threat to the Church's freedom, and the political administration gave more recognition to Catholic interests and aspirations than any in history. Men like John Ryan believed that the time had come for Catholics to take their place in the authentic American mainstream now enshrined in the reform administration of Franklin Roosevelt. But many were less sure. Catholic influence on the New Deal was minimal; Roosevelt did seem on occasion to ignore Catholic sensibilities, and the nation's most ardent New Dealers came from the ranks of sophisticated eastern liberals who some Catholics had always regarded as more potent enemies than southern and western fundamentalists. The word "liberal" was a badge of honor for John Ryan, representing to him a position consistent with Catholic natural rights philosophy, the same philosophy which underlay American freedoms. For many others, however, the word summed up the elements in American society they most feared, elements which threatened the autonomy of the Church and challenged the American practices they had always considered most essential.

For those who adopted the latter position, the real establishment in America was not a plutocratic oligarchy, as Ryan seemed to believe, but a liberal elite composed of professors, editors, labor leaders, politicians, and, for some, Jews. The Church remained a besieged garrison, in need of discipline, unity, and vigilance, but her role was not one of simple defense; she had a mission to Christianize and at the same time "re-Americanize" America, an effort sanctioned by the hierarchy's proclamation of a "Catholic Crusade for Christian Democracy" in 1938. The assumptions that shaped this view of the Church in America were clarified by Father Francis X. Talbot, editor of *America*. Talbot was convinced that Catholics were the largest group in the nation still adhering "to the Constitution and the traditional Americanism that made our country what it was before 1914." Given cohesion by their doctrinal and disciplinary unity, Catholics thought in "almost identical patterns [on] all other matters, social, economic, ethical, moral, cultural (but not political)." Sure that they could "furnish the answer to every national question" Catholics constituted "a tremendous national force" wholly opposed to "the changes coming over American civilization," changes resulting from "American liberals . . . being infected with un-American ideas and the American proletariat being mobilized for redress."

Talbot's view of the Church's situation in the United States was not unusual; many others urged a united "Catholic front" to promote Church interests and teachings, to spread acceptance of Christian moral principles, and defend democratic ideas and institutions against communism and secularism. Education was seen as a crucial battlefield, more critical indeed than national politics. In 1940 the National Catholic Alumni Federation sponsored a symposium on the topic "Man and Modern Secularism." Most of the speakers identified Catholic educational practices with American traditions and denounced secular and progressive education as both unchristian and un-American. The President of Fordham University charged that American public schools were pervaded by a secularism which denied or ignored the supernatural and "degraded" man "to the level of nature." Historians Richard Purcell and Richard Gabel described denominational influence on colonial and early national schools, "a Catholic position on religion in education," which had been destroyed when secularism was "foisted upon American education largely through the adoption of non-sectarian religion." Geoffrey O'Connell, author of *Naturalism in American Education*, described the "atheist" doctrines of the National Educational Association and of leading professors at Columbia Teachers College, while Thomas Woodlock charged that non-Catholic students, because of their lack of religious training, could not defend the principles of the Declaration of Independence. Other speakers went on to praise the Catholic educational system, to urge its extension, and to point out its importance as a force in preserving true American values.

Only a few took issue with the dominant tone of the discussions. Professor Ross Hoffman warned against regarding the advent of a lay society as necessarily harmful to the Church, whose mission was "not to clericalize, but to catholicize society, using whatever means . . . are available to that sublime end." In a lay civilization this meant the sanctification of souls by forming men capable of creative work in the various "secular" areas of human activity, a theme elaborated by Robert C. Pollock, who charged that Catholics were "as one-sided as the secularists." They "one-sidedly affirm the spiritual," Pollock argued, while others "one-sidedly affirm the temporal," at a time when the great need was a reconciliation of the two. Drawing upon traditional Catholic sources he urged a more positive approach to modern life and defended "secularism" as "the temporal order . . . striving after its own rightful form, motivated by the Christian impulse towards the affirmation of the creature and its autonomy." Particularly in America it was imperative that Catholics abandon their condemnations and seek to affirm all values, "wheresoever they be found, in heaven or on earth." Only thus could Catholics "pay off their debt to the modern world for their failures in the past."

Pollock was one of the few American Catholics in the decade to inter-
pret America's challenge to the Church in a manner similar to Hecker
and Ireland in the previous century. Economic abundance and political
freedom in the United States for the first time made possible the realization in concrete form of the Christian ideal of brotherhood and equality.
"When Christianity came into the world the wall of separation between
man and man was doomed," Pollock wrote. "American democracy represents in the temporal order man's determination to destroy this wall of
separation. Because men are men, we must construct a social order that
will emphasize and strengthen, not the differences that divide men, but
the common humanity which unites them." America possessed the tech-
nical skill and material resources to end the struggle for existence and
challenged the Church to forge powerful links with the people and work
for the temporal realization of its belief in equality and human dignity.

This view of the positive relation between Christiainty and Americanism was not a popular one in the 1930's. By the end of the decade
many regarded the dominant trends of their time as antithetical to the
doctrines of their Church and the ideals of their nation. The difference
between the two positions pivoted upon an assessment of the contemporary scene, and that evaluation was shaped by sociological more than
doctrinal factors. Just as acceptance of the Christian social order brought
no consensus on policies or programs, neither did acceptance of "true
Americanism" result in any monolithic commitment to particular features
of American life and thought. For Americanism, like Catholic social doctrine, turned out to be a magician's hat that produced pre-packaged rab-
bits. Reformers and conservatives, friends and enemies of the Supreme
Court, isolationists and internationalists, all found justification for their
positions by reference to what they regarded as accurate interpretations
of papal thought and valid references to the authentic American tradition. In the decade the more negative stance dominated Catholic life,
despite the efforts of men like John Ryan, George Shuster, Francis Haas,
and others to keep open the lines of communication between Catholics
and other Americans and to mobilize Catholic support for efforts by men
of good will to improve the quality of American society.

There remained still a third option for American Catholics: rejection
of America, in theory and in fact, in favor of a wholehearted commitment to Christian truths transcending the limits of geography, nation,

ethnic group, and social class. Before the 1930's this position had been taken only by a small group of Catholic corporatists who understood the antiliberal social philosophy that underlay the social thought of continental Catholicism that ultimately found expression in *Quadragesimo Anno*. Agreeing that America needed to be Christianized, they denied that this could be accomplished by relying on American traditions. Frederick Kenkel, Edward Koch, and others who held this position, belittled the New Deal's efforts to save liberal capitalism, and they attacked moderate Catholics who sought to reconcile the organic, functional theory of Christian social thought with the chaotic individualism of American political and economic life. Relying on education, they patiently awaited the failure of such palliatives as social legislation and trade unionism, confident that eventually, to save itself from totalitarianism or anarchy, America would pay them heed.

In a quite different way the new group of radical Catholics who appeared in the 1930's refused to look for a root Americanism with which to identify. Led by Paul Hanley Furfey, Peter Maurin, and Dorothy Day, they attacked the anxiety of Catholics to be fully Americanized and urged them instead to "think Catholic answers to every problem of their lives." They deplored the influence of American Protestantism and individualism on Catholics whose loyalty to the Church was often coupled with submission to the social and cultural standards of non-Catholic America. Like the Americanizers they fought separatism and aloofness, but because it was unchristian, not because it was un-American. Rather than striving to win recognition and praise, they urged Catholics to "promote the uncompromising advance of supernatural Catholicism along every sector of the Catholic front and around every side of Catholic individual and social life." Such an approach would build a truly Catholic culture, win converts, and lead to personalist social action which would revolutionize American society.

This perfectionism provided a solid basis for self-criticism within the Catholic community and directly challenged the implicit self-righteousness of much Catholic opinion. Instead of focusing on the nation's abandonment of its ideals, the lay Catholics who followed Furfey, Maurin, and Dorothy Day, concentrated on the Catholic community's own failure to live up to the standards it professed. But, like the group-oriented approach of Father Talbot, this desire for an integral Catholicism often appeared to assume that the Church did possess answers to all American problems, that there were social and cultural forms that would fully express Christian beliefs, that there were such things as a Catholic society and a Catholic position on every aspect of life. If all this was true there was no question that Catholics should unite to promote specifically Catholic objectives in social and political life. However, a few like Pollock and Hoffman were questioning this assumption at the end of the decade. Virgil Michel, for example, disagreed with the contention that Catholics should think alike on nonreligious matters. "As Catholics we agree on essentials of faith and morals," Michel wrote.

> But there is no earthly (or heavenly) reason why we must all agree on any other questions, including public questions. Quite the contrary. If, as some seem to hold, we should, in spite of legitimate differences, put on a 'united front,' pretending to agree on every other detailed question, would we not be as the scribes and pharisees. . . .

Nevertheless, most American Catholic intellectuals held fast to the belief that there were specifically Catholic answers to most of life's problems that should serve as the basis for a mass Catholic social movement. Michel, Hoffman, and Pollock, along with the Catholic Worker's leaders, only began to question this belief and to lay the basis for a new approach to Catholic life in America, which would not become powerful for another generation.

For almost two centuries the conditions of what German theologian Karl Rahner calls "the diaspora" had been developing in the United States. Dependence on lay support, lack of cultural dominance, and separation of Church and State were basic features of American religious life. To be sure Americans long regarded their nation as "made by Protestants and cast in a Protestant mold," but their experience and their institutions denied the age-old belief that social and cultural coherence must be based on religious uniformity. The emergence in the twentieth century of large organized blocs of Catholics, Jews, and nonbelievers forced the unfolding of the logic of the American situation, resulting in a real religious pluralism. For American Catholics these same conditions raised the problem of adjusting the claims of religious authority to the demands of a free society and secular State, forcing them to challenge the belief, so strong in the Old World, that "Catholicism could not survive in a *milieu* which did not pay it homage." Whether the need to find a non-religious basis of social integration resulted in "an idolatrous new religion of Americanism," a "uniform, middle class, liberal secularism," or merely a consensus on political practices which removed ultimate values from the realm of public debate, American Catholics faced a diaspora more clearly defined than elsewhere in the world.

At the end of a decade of controversy, American Catholicism's response to the challenges of American voluntarism remained in many respects unchanged. To be sure there was increased diversity in the Catholic community, and it was less possible to speak of American Catholics as a bloc than it had been in 1929. In addition, there was an increased interest in political and social matters and the influence of Catholics on American life was increasing. But most of the characteristics of American Catholicism remained those of the ghetto, which Rahner describes as the natural reaction to the coming of the diaspora.

> What, after all, does a person do if he sees the diaspora situation coming and thinks of it as something which simply and absolutely cannot be? He makes himself a closed circle, an artificial situation inside which it looks as if the internal and outward diaspora isn't one; he makes a ghetto. . . . Here we are, all together, and we can behave as though there were nothing in the world but Christians.

The critic who wished to generalize might have found it more difficult in 1940 than a decade earlier, but he could present solid evidence that the Church remained unusually rigid in its hierarchical structure and still quite narrow in social outlook. The passionate, self-righteous identification of Catholicism and Americanism, the preoccupation with questions of private and public morality, the willingness to use power to impose Christian teachings on society, and the occasional tendency to place institutional interests above the common good remained unpleasant realities in American Catholic life.

Even the more liberal Catholics remained within boundaries that appear narrow a generation later. They fully agreed on the doctrinal and moral teachings of the Church and never criticized efforts to obtain public recognition of Christian moral standards through the pressure group activities of the Legion of Decency or the demands for prohibitive statutes against birth control propaganda. Within the Church all Catholic spokesmen accepted the products of the Church's history in the United States, defended the parochial schools and the numerous Catholic organizations, and acknowledged the role of the bishops and the need for obedience in ill-defined but broad areas of life. On economic matters too there were boundaries around the sharpest controversy. No important Catholic figure challenged the doctrine of private property or rejected the wage system and few seriously questioned the acceptability of profits and competition, so long as they were limited by the demands of the common good. All supported the program of Pius XI, endorsing the occupational group system and agreeing that justice and charity were the moral and practical guides for reform. Although some Catholics might have doubted the wisdom of the emphasis chosen by some of their leaders, none questioned the importance of opposing communism or striving to provide a religious basis for Americanism by fighting the spread of secularism in all areas of American life.

The exploration of the meaning of work in an industrial society, the awareness of the problems of community and fellowship in modern times, the willingness of many to co-operate with non-Catholics, even with Communists, in securing legitimate objectives, the emphasis upon human dignity and freedom rather than on formal and abstract notions of a Christian social order or negative ideals of anticommunism and defense of the Church—these aspects of Catholic thought in the thirties were important foreshadowings of future developments, but in the decade they remained novelties, overshadowed by the more negative aspects of Catholic life and thought. The desire of the people around the Catholic Worker movement to live fully Christian lives and to find social structures conducive to the realization of personal responsibility and personal dignity was less characteristic of American Catholicism than was the desire to be fully Catholic and fully American without having to confront the realities of either. This desire for a monolithic American Catholicism and an equally integrated Catholic Americanism could be seen in the sharp and bitter reaction of many to George Shuster's attempt at dialogue with American liberals, the sudden loss of circulation by *Commonweal* when it abandoned the Franco cause, the bitter letters that were sent to John Ryan after he attacked Father Coughlin and after he defended the "court-packing" plan, and the collapse of the *Catholic Worker*'s popularity when it refused to abandon pacifism after Pearl Harbor.

Nevertheless American Catholicism did show signs of a new maturity and creativity during the 1930's. The hierarchy, while remaining essentially conservative, did succeed for a time in overcoming the restrictions of Catholic history and presenting a humane and charitable response to the suffering and misery occasioned by unemployment and economic stagnation. Individual bishops appeared who showed foresight and courage in supporting economic reform, labor unions, and social welfare legislation and opposing reaction and isolation within the Catholic community. Many clergymen were willing to depart from strictly parochial concerns to assist their congregations to secure a wider measure of social justice. A few bishops, priests, and laymen began to direct mild criticism at Catholic complacency and self-righteousness. These words seemed to have little effect at the time, but they began a process that would accelerate in the years that followed the war.

Perhaps the most significant aspect of Catholic life in the thirties was the appearance of an awakened laity anxious to realize Christian values in secular life without insisting on uniformity of belief or adherence to the Church. Before the Depression it was possible to speak of American Catholicism almost entirely in terms of the hierarchy and clergy—that is, in terms of the institutional Church as it had developed since the trusteeism episode of the early nineteenth century. In the thirties, however, a significant number of lay Catholics, unable to find meaning and satisfaction in strictly parochial and ethnic organizations, independently sought to find new ways of realizing their religious commitments in their personal lives, at the same time attempting to make Catholicism meaningful within American society.

The Catholic Worker movement, numerically small as it was, presented an effective challenge to the life of American Catholics. From their different backgrounds Dorothy Day and Peter Maurin brought to the American Church a sense of unity of men and of the personal responsibility of each man for the welfare of all. Like the IWW she had known in her youth Dorothy Day proclaimed that "an injury to one is an injury to all." From such a standard, supported by the theological concept of the Mystical Body of Christ, the *Catholic Worker* could criticize and challenge American Catholicism on its own grounds of brotherhood and Christian love. It could and did demonstrate to the layman that his desire for social justice and personal involvement could be realized within the

Catholic fold. The movement's pioneering interest in religious art, liturgical reform, advanced theological and philosophical speculation, and radical social change, demonstrated the potential richness of the Catholic tradition and anticipated the events of the 1960's. Sensitive laymen had often rebelled against the shallowness and sterility of the cultural milieu of their youth and had felt compelled to leave the Church of their fathers in order to realize their desire for creative activity, intellectual honesty, and personal fulfillment. After the 1930's the situation would no longer be as clear, for the laymen of the *Catholic Worker, Commonweal,* and numerous minor journals and organizations, effectively demonstrated that the Catholic Church could offer far more space, far more depth, and far more freedom than Americans, including Catholics, had suspected.

American Catholics and the Intellectual Life

JOHN TRACY ELLIS

Since World War II Catholics have made very rapid strides toward social and economic parity with other Americans, and their religion has gained acceptance as one of the "three great faiths" that underpin the American Way of Life. As they upgraded themselves to middle-class status in a period of sustained prosperity, Catholics lost interest in the issues of social and economic reform that had engaged them along with other Americans in the Depression years. In place of these concerns, Catholics became painfully aware that their contributions to the intellectual and cultural life of the nation were in no way commensurate with their numbers. Thus there was in the 1950s an outpouring of self-criticism. Catholic writers castigated their parochial schools and colleges, lamented the dearth of Catholic scientists and scholars, and made a sort of general confession of sins against "intellectualism." By far the most influential and widely read piece of self-criticism was the essay reprinted below, "American Catholics and the Intellectual Life," by John Tracy Ellis. Its impact derived not only from its detailed exposition of the Catholic record of intellectual backwardness, but also from the prestige of the author. Monsignor Ellis, then Professor of American Church History at the Catholic University of America and author of a monumental biography of Cardinal Gibbons, was the foremost historian of American Catholicism. Now Professor of Church History at the University of San Francisco, Monsignor Ellis has been uniquely successful among American Catholic scholars in bringing his great learning to bear on issues of contemporary interest.

John Tracy Ellis, "American Catholics and the Intellectual Life," *Thought,* XXX (Autumn, 1955), pp. 353-358, 360-372, 374-378, 385-386. Reprinted with deletions and without footnotes by permission of the author and the publisher.

IN 1941] ONE OF THE MOST PERCEPTIVE OF LIVING FOREIGN OBSERV-
ers of American life and institutions, Denis W. Brogan, professor of
political science in the University of Cambridge, stated in a book on
the United States: ". . . in no Western society is the intellectual prestige of
Catholicism lower than in the country where, in such respects as wealth,
numbers, and strength of organization, it is so powerful." No well-in-
formed American Catholic will attempt to challenge that statement. Ad-
mittedly, the weakest aspect of the Church in this country lies in its
failure to produce national leaders and to exercise commanding influence
in intellectual circles, and this at a time when the number of Catholics in
the United States is exceeded only by those of Brazil and Italy, and their
material resources are incomparably superior to those of any other branch
of the universal Church. What, one may ask, is the explanation of this
striking discrepancy? The remainder of this paper will be devoted to an
attempt to answer that question by a development of certain major points
based, for the most part, on the history of the American Church.

The first point, namely, the implanting in this soil of a deep anti-
Catholic prejudice by the original English settlers in the early seventeenth
century, requires no elaborate proof for any educated American. One has
but to read the exhaustive monograph of Sister Mary Augustina Ray,
B.V.M., on eighteenth-century America, or the general work of Gustavus
Myers, to understand how thoroughly hostile to all things Catholic great
numbers of Americans have always been, and the pains that they have
taken to perpetuate that bias since it first entered the stream of American
history at Jamestown and Plymouth Rock. In the spring of 1942 I had
the fact brought home to me in a forceful way when Professor Arthur
M. Schlesinger, Sr., of Harvard University, one of the outstanding authorities in American social history, remarked to me during a friendly chat in
Cambridge, "I regard the bias against your Church as the most persistent
prejudice in the history of the American people." Any notion that this
sentiment was only a part of our past has been thoroughly dispelled by
the substantial support afforded to groups like the Protestants and Other
Americans United for Separation of Church and State since World
War II.

Historically speaking, therefore, the American intellectual climate has been aloof and unfriendly to Catholic thought and ideas, when it has not been openly hostile, and it places no burden upon the imagination to appreciate how this factor has militated against a strong and vibrant intellectual life among the Catholics of this country. All but the most sanguine of men feel discouragement in circumstances of this kind and the majority usually give way to the natural tendency to slacken their efforts. What is more serious, the presence of so widespread a prejudice among the great majority of the population prompts the minority to withdraw into itself and to assume the attitude of defenders of a besieged fortress. That this situation had such an effect on many Catholics, there is no doubt. Even so brave and talented a man as John Carroll, the first American Catholic bishop, revealed the timidity engendered among the Catholics of his day by hatred of their Church when he was compelled to go into print in 1784 to refute a subtle attack on Catholic doctrine from the first American apostate priest. As Carroll remarked, "I could not forget, in the beginning, progress, and conclusion of it, that the habits of thinking, the prejudices, perhaps even the passions of many of my readers, would be set against all the arguments I could offer. . . ." How many Catholics since Carroll's day could attest to the same reluctance when they sought to exercise their talents in behalf of Catholic truth? And yet anti-Catholic bias should not be advanced as the prime factor in this situation. More damaging than its direct effect on the intellectual shortcomings of American Catholics, has probably been the fostering by this historic bias of an overeagerness in Catholic circles for apologetics rather than pure scholarship.

A second major consideration which helps to account for the failure of American Catholics to make a notable mark upon the intellectual life of their country is the character and background of the major portion of the people who, until a relatively recent date, made up the Church in the United States. From the 1820's, when the Irish began immigrating to the new world in large numbers, to the 1920's, when Congress locked the doors upon all but a small proportion of the immigrants who sought these shores, the Catholic Church was faced with the staggering task of absorbing an estimated 9,317,000 immigrants of its faith. We do not need to be told what the immigrant status implied by way of poverty, hardship, yes, and even illiteracy. Most of us learned it from tales told by our grandparents within the intimacy of the family circle. And since we have had the advantage of a finished education and know what that requires, we can easily understand how impossible it was for our ancestors to produce anything approaching a thriving intellectual life. Moreover, the grave responsibility that these unceasing waves of immigrants imposed upon the leaders of the Church to see that they had the rudiments of religious instruction and the facilities for Mass and the sacraments, left little time, funds, or leisure for a more highly cultivated training. Brogan understands that fact. In 1941 he wrote:

> Not until this generation has the Church been given time (with the cessation of mass immigration) to take breath and take stock. One result of this preoccupation with the immigrants has been that the Catholic Church in America has counted for astonishingly little in the formation of the American intellectual climate. . . .

It is only the exceptional man—for example, John Gilmary Shea, the historian of the American Church—who can make headway in the world of scholarship amid crippling poverty and the harassing anxiety of providing a living for himself and his dependents. That was the lot of most of the Catholics in this country in Shea's generation and before, and that there should have resulted a pitifully meager record of accomplishments in the things of the mind is thus quite understandable.

But even if the energies of the American Catholic body down to a generation ago had not been so completely absorbed in the primary duty of assimilating the millions of immigrants, any true intellectual distinction—had it been there—would have met with very slight appreciation in the United States. Historically, Americans have been wary of their scholars, and it is doubtful if there is a major nation in the world whose history reveals more suspicion of its academicians than our own. It is now 120 years since de Tocqueville published his famous book on American institutions, and among his many wise observations he stated:

> In the United States the people do not hate the higher classes of society, but are not favorably inclined towards them and carefully exclude them from the exercise of authority. They do not fear distinguished talents, but are rarely fond of them. In general, everyone who rises without their aid seldom obtains their favor.

The prevalence of this egalitarian spirit and the leveling process which it inspired prompted Orestes Brownson to inveigh against the American practice of dethroning all distinction when he delivered the commencement address at Mount Saint Mary's College in 1853. On that occasion he pleaded with the graduates to resist with might and main this tendency which he characterized as "the grand heresy of our age." Nor have matters greatly improved since the time of de Tocqueville and Brownson, for it has been our own generation that has given birth to the terms "brain trusters" and "egg heads" to designate the popular concept of professors who have descended from Mount Olympus to engage actively in the realm of public affairs.

In this respect, I regret to say, I can see no appreciable difference between the attitudes assumed by American Catholics and those commonly held among their fellow countrymen of other religious faiths. The historian looks in vain—always excepting the lonely few—for a higher evaluation and a more understanding attitude toward the pursuits of the mind among those who are Catholics in this country. In that—as in so many other ways—the Catholics are, and have been, thoroughly American, and they have shown no more marked disposition to foster scholarship and to honor intellectual achievement than have any other group. . . .

One of the principal reasons for the lack of such an exception is, I think, the absence of an intellectual tradition among American Catholics. Obviously the establishment of such a tradition was impossible amid the stifling persecution and discrimination which Catholics experienced in colonial America. With the dawn of religious liberty after the American Revolution there was a brief span of years when it seemed that a tradition of this kind was slowly taking root among the families of the Maryland Catholic gentry. For the personal wealth of some of these families like the Carrolls, the Neales, and the Brookes, along with their deep and ardent Catholic faith, had enabled them to send their children to Europe where they acquired an education that was second to none among Americans of their generation. Moreover, when the French Revolution had turned violently anticlerical in the 1790's there came to this country a large number of highly cultivated French priests who exercised a strong and uplifting influence upon the intellectual life of the small and beleagured Catholic body. One has but to recall the names of François Matignon, Jean Cheverus, Simon Bruté, Benedict Flager, and Gabriel Richard—all men of a finished education, fine personal libraries, and a deep love of learning—to know what is meant. But before this high promise of the early nineteenth century had time to attain fulfillment the arrival of the great mass of immigrants dissipated the early hope for intellectual distinction which faded away before the all-important task of saving souls.

As the mid-century approached, it is true, there came another ray of hope when a small band of intellectual converts afforded a temporary expectation that the American Church might witness an Oxford Movement of its own. Within the single decade of the 1840's Orestes Brownson, Augustine Hewit, Isaac Hecker, Anna Hanson Dorsey, George Allen, Clarence Walworth, James Roosevelt Bayley, Jedidiah Huntington, William Henry Anderson, and Joseph Chandler found their way into the Church. They were all native-born Americans of prominent families, most of them had received the best American education of their time in predominantly Protestant schools, and practically all of them were of a literary turn of mind and might be termed intellectuals. They did, indeed, lift the intellectual tone of Catholicism in this country. But the predominant cast had already been given to the religious society they now entered, and the fact that in the decade of their conversion the immigrant population accounted for 700,000 out of the 1,660,000 Catholics in the country by 1850, would explain in good measure the relatively slight impression which this little band of converts made upon the intellectual life of the vast majority of their coreligionists. With the latter the all-absorbing ambition was to find a livelihood and to make the minimum of necessary adjustments to their new environment. In the end the native-born converts with their thoroughly American background were no more successful than the European-educated and European-born Catholics of an earlier generation in establishing a lasting intellectual tradition.

It was the conviction of the need for a tradition of this kind in the American Church that inspired some of the finest passages of the sermon preached by John Lancaster Spalding, Bishop of Peoria, during the Third Plenary Council of Baltimore. To Spalding the time was long overdue for the Catholics of this country to stand forth and give the lie to the inherited prejudice of millions of Americans that the Church was the mother of ignorance. Catholic conduct during the nation's wars, he remarked, had convinced all but the most unreasonable of the depth and sincerity of their patriotism. But in the intellectual order, it was another matter. Thus said Spalding:

when our zeal for intellectual excellence shall have raised up men who will take place among the first writers and thinkers of their day their very presence will become the most persuasive of arguments to teach the world that no best gift is at war with the spirit of Catholic faith. . . .

Five years later at the centennial of the American hierarchy John Ireland, Archbishop of St. Paul, made a similar plea to the Catholics of the United States to strive for leadership in intellectual circles. He stated:

> This is an intellectual age. It worships intellect. It tries all things by the touchstone of intellect. . . . The Church herself will be judged by the standard of intellect. Catholics must excel in religious knowledge. . . . They must be in the foreground of intellectual movements of all kinds. The age will not take kindly to religious knowledge separated from secular knowledge.

Yet in spite of the stirring pleas of bishops like Spalding and Ireland, and of the constant and heroic efforts of editors like Brownson in his *Quarterly Review,* of Hecker in the *Catholic World,* and of James A. Corcoran in the *American Catholic Quarterly Review,* the vast majority of Catholics remained relatively impervious to the intellectual movements of their time. A fact which demonstrates clearly the failure of an intellectual tradition to have taken root among them up to the closing years of the last century relates to the Catholic University of America. When the American hierarchy opened the University in November, 1889, the native-born Catholics of this country were so devoid of scholarly distinction that the first rector, John J. Keane, was compelled to recruit his original faculty of eight men from among six foreign-born professors and two American-born converts. One could scarcely find a more striking illustration of intellectual impoverishment than this, especially when it is remembered that Bishop Keane had sought in every way possible to avoid the charge of "foreignism" which groups like the A.P.A. were then leveling against his infant institution.

One of the main reasons why the American Church after a century of organized existence in the United States found itself with no intellectual tradition was, I am convinced again, due to the character and background of its adherents. Had there been a sufficiently large number of American Catholic families with several generations of a solid tradition and love of learning in their midst, the appeals of men like Brownson and Spalding might, indeed, have borne more fruit. The La Farge family is a case in point. In the correspondence of John La Farge, the artist, during his school days at Mount Saint Mary's College in Emmitsburg one finds, for example, that before La Farge had reached his sixteenth birthday he had in the course of two and a half months requested his father to send him works of Herodotus, Plautus, Catullus, Theocritus, Dryden, Goldsmith, Michelet, Molière, Corneille, and Victor Hugo. And that the love of books acquired by the great artist was passed on to his children, was recently witnessed when his Jesuit son published his interesting memoirs and described how seriously reading was taken in the La Farge household. There his uncle, Thomas Sergeant Perry, professor of English at Harvard, his father, and his mother read regularly to the children from the best books. Out of habits such as these there developed a taste for good literature and Father La Farge tells us:

> One day in August when I was about thirteen, I finished devouring Boswell's *Life of Johnson* and a feeling of desolation came over me as I turned the last page. . . . Then the bright idea occurred to me, why not read the two fat volumes through again? It was a wise choise and I shall never regret it.

That is the kind of background from which true intellectuals are born, but how many American Catholic families are there of whom that could be said? . . .

It is a sad fact but, I think, a true one that on the whole American Catholic families have largely failed in this regard, just as the families of Americans generally have failed. The tradition that established itself in the La Farge family circle has never enjoyed wide acceptance in Catholic households, and when an attempt to foster such a tradition is sometimes made in Catholic institutions of higher education it is often found that the effort has come too late.

But the lack of serious reading habits is not the only national characteristic which the Catholics of the United States have thoroughly imbibed. From the time when the Duc de Liancourt traveled through the states along the eastern seaboard in the 1790's and wrote one of the earliest books by a foreigner on the new Republic, to the essays of recent observers like Evelyn Waugh, few visitors from abroad have neglected to comment on the American attachment to material goods and the desire to make a fortune as dominant characteristics of our society. . . .

Here, too, the prevailing American ethos took captive the Catholics as well as those affiliated with other churches. In no single phase of national life have Catholics made the contribution to leadership which might be expected of them, but if there be any exception to this general statement, it almost certainly lies in the field of business. For example, six years ago William Miller of Harvard made a study of 187 business leaders and 163 political leaders for the first ten years of the twentieth century. In neither category were the Catholics distinguished, but it is worthy of note that they comprised almost double (7 per cent) the number of leaders in business that they did in politics (4 per cent) during the years 1900-1910. A similar investigation by Liston Pope, professor of social ethics in Yale University, which centered around the years 1939-1946 tended to bear out the same conclusion. In this case a scrutiny of the relation between the religious affiliation and economic status of Protestants and Catholics at the opening of the 1940's led to the equally interesting observation that, "Protestantism had a larger representation from the lower class and Catholicism had more middle-class members than popular generalizations have assumed." In other words, Catholics have moved up the economic ladder beyond the rung where popular impression had placed them.

I was sufficiently intrigued by the data contained in these articles to institute an investigation among the students of my seminar on the subject of Catholic leadership in the three fields of business, politics, and scholarship during the 1940's. Their findings were, of course, quite tentative in nature, but they did indicate that, relatively speaking, Catholic business leadership on a national scale in those years ran ahead of leadership in national politics, and it made the showing by Catholics who had attained national recognition through productive scholarship seem insignificant by comparison. There is, then, warrant for saying that Catholics have not only shown an increasing participation in the native penchant for making money, but that, all things considered, they have probably attained more distinction in the business world than they have in any other sector of American life.

But has the arrival of a fairly large number of American Catholic business men at the status of millionaires—many of whom are college graduates—occasioned any notable change in their attitude toward or increase in their support of the intellectual pursuits of their coreligionists? That question brings us to the sixth major point which I should like to make, namely, the failure of Catholics in posts of leadership, both clerical and lay, to understand fully, or to appreciate in a practical way, the value of the vocation of the intellectual. First, to return to the question of the laity, the answer is not, I believe, a clear Yes or an unqualified No. About the only norm of judgment that one can apply to their attitude, unless one knows them personally, is their outward action in the form of endowments of the things of the mind. In that respect one can say that the situation at present reveals a higher appreciation of intellectual values on the part of Catholics of wealth than it did two generations ago when, to be sure, the number possessing large fortunes was much smaller. . . .

. . . All things considered, the last two decades have seen improvement in the financial support given to intellectual enterprises by Catholics of wealth in this country. Furthermore, the current awareness which many American business leaders are demonstrating of their responsibility toward higher education is a happy augury, and it gives rise to the hope that the Catholics among them will now step forward and identify themselves strongly with this movement. The Knights of Columbus have given them a splendid example by their recent gift to Saint Louis University for the microfilming of the manuscripts in the Vatican Library, a benefaction which will prove of inestimable value to the prestige and future possibilities of American Catholic scholarship. To date, however, it may be truly said that the over-all record of intelligent appreciation and high evaluation for the intellectual activities of their Church on the part of wealthy Catholic lay leaders has not been an impressive one.

• • •

That brings us to the role played by the clerical leaders of the American Church. In anything that is said or written on the subject of either the clerical or lay leaders in the Church of the United States it should be constantly kept in mind that, *mutatis mutandis,* the vast majority of them have been men of their own generation, reflecting—apart from the dogmatic and moral views which they held as Catholics—the predominant attitudes and prevailing tendencies of their time. . . . [T]he bishops and major superiors of the religious orders of this generation reveal, it seems to me, the characteristics of their time, for among them one will find men whose executive and administrative talents are of a very high order. It is fortunate that this is so, for it is no exaggeration to say that the

Catholic Church of the United States has become "big business" in the typically American meaning of that term. And, we may add, woe to Catholic interests if the bishops and the heads of the principal religious orders were not men who possessed the ability to cope with the problems that the far-flung commitments of the American Church now daily impose upon them!

Yet it is to be regretted that the pressing tasks of administration leave so little time and leisure to these spiritual superiors for a more active participation and effective encouragement to intellectual concerns. Their backgrounds do not account for the lack of it, for they are basically the same as that of the Catholic intellectuals themselves. That point was made clear by Archbishop Cushing in 1947 when he stated to the ninth annual convention of the C.I.O. meeting in his see city:

> I have said this before, but it is important to repeat it here: in all the American hierarchy, resident in the United States, there is not known to me one Bishop, Archbishop or Cardinal whose father or mother was a college graduate. Every one of our Bishops and Archbishops is the son of a working man and a working man's wife.

Many of these prelates of whom the Archbishop of Boston spoke are, of course, themselves college graduates, and a considerable number of them are the products of graduate training in fields like theology, philosophy, canon law, education, and social work. To be sure, these are not *per se* fields of vocational training, but there has been a strong tendency to make them that. On the other hand, relatively few of the higher clergy have taken graduate work in the humanities and the liberal arts. As a consequence one will find among them, I believe, a far greater emphasis on what are the professional and vocational aspects of higher education, since they serve a practical end in their diocesan chanceries, charities, and offices of the superintendents of schools, than might otherwise be the case. In this, I submit, they faithfully mirror the intense preoccupation of American leaders in all walks of life with the practical. That the practical order of things is of vital importance to the Church, no one with any understanding of its mission would attempt to deny. But by the same token the Church has a mission to the intellectual elite and this, I fear, has been allowed to suffer neglect by reason of the prevalence of the practical.

Apart, however, from personal backgrounds, the harassing day-to-day duties of administration, and the national temper of practicality which bishops and religious superiors—like all the rest of us—have imbibed as an influencing factor in their lives, the churchmen have not been able to draw upon a well-established intellectual tradition inherited from the countries of their origin. The majority of these men have been of Irish or German extraction, and by virtue of similarity of language and customs many of them have closely followed developments of the Church in England. In neither the Ireland nor the Germany of their grandparents and parents; nor in the England that they have observed since the conversion of Newman in 1845, have they found such a tradition. . . .

Moreover, the failure of American churchmen to find guidance and inspiration from a strong intellectual tradition in the lands of their ancestors was in no way compensated by the training they received in preparation for their priesthood, whether that be in diocesan seminaries or in the scholasticates of the religious orders. As Bishop [John Lancaster] Spalding stated at the Third Plenary Council of Baltimore: ". . . the ecclesiastical seminary is not a school of intellectual culture, either here in America or elsewhere, and to imagine that it can become the instrument of intellectual culture is to cherish a delusion. . . ." Spalding rightly maintained that the seminary was, and must necessarily be, a training school for a profession, albeit a profession that might be expected to have more than an ordinary kinship for intellectual pursuits. But I wonder very much if the seminaries and scholasticates of our religious orders have made the most of their opportunities for intellectual stimulation and the cultivation of serious reading habits in their students that they should have. Speaking of the failure of the American priest to be more intellectually alive, John Talbot Smith, a respected New York priest, said nearly sixty years ago something which prompts one to ask if it is not still substantially true. He wrote:

> The habits of the intellectual life in the seminary have dwarfed him. The curriculum rarely recognizes anything but theology and philosophy, and these often isolated from present conditions and without practical knowledge. . . . [and] . . . History is taught in random, unscientific fashion, to judge the method by the results. . . . It is not then a cause for wonder that the young priest should graduate so rude and unfinished. The wonder is that he should at all be able to hold his own in the sneering world, so skilled in knowledge of its times, so devoted to science and history. . . .

Smith placed a good deal of responsibility on the hierarchy for the low state of intellectual endeavor among the priests of his generation, maintaining that to bring the entire educational system of the Church up to the mark was, as he said, "clearly the work of the episcopate, and no other power with which the church in America is acquainted can do that work." Furthermore, he made it quite clear that he had in mind the religious orders as well as the diocesan priests, for with the religious superiors, too, he felt that only the bishops could bring about a change.

It may well be that Father Smith placed too heavy a burden of blame on the bishops of his day for the failure to foster a higher intellectual life among the clergy. But that their example and influence in these matters can exert a powerful influence in the lives of their subjects, is beyond question. I happen to have been born in the Diocese of Peoria, and I knew at first hand the imprint left by Bishop John Lancaster Spalding on the intellectual tastes, the good reading, and the careful preparation of sermons of many of his priests. It was a subject for comment when I was growing up, and I could personally verify from an acquaintance with several of these venerable priests the effect that these intellectual habits had upon their lives.

* * *

Part of the reason why American Catholics have not made a notable impression on the intellectual life of their country is due, I am convinced, to what might be called a betrayal of that which is peculiarly their own. The nature of that betrayal has been highlighted during the last quarter of a century by such movements as the scholastic revival in philosophy which found its most enthusiastic and hard-working friends on the campuses of the University of Chicago, the University of Virginia, Princeton University, and St. John's College, Annapolis. Meanwhile the Catholic universities were engrossed in their mad pursuit of every passing fancy that crossed the American educational scene, and found relatively little time for distinguished contributions to scholastic philosophy. Woefully lacking in the endowment, training, and equipment to make them successful competitors of the secular universities in fields like engineering, business administration, nursing education, and the like, the Catholic universities, nonetheless, went on multiplying these units and spreading their budgets so thin—in an attempt to include everything—that the subjects in which they could, and should, make a unique contribution were sorely neglected.

That American educators expect Catholic institutions to be strong in the humanities and the liberal arts—to say nothing of theology and philosophy—is not surprising. Eighteen years ago Robert M. Hutchins, then President of the University of Chicago, in an address before the Middle West regional unit of the National Catholic Educational Association made that point in a very forceful way. Speaking of the Catholic Church as having what he called "the longest intellectual tradition of any institution in the contemporary world," Hutchins criticized the Catholic institutions for failing to emphasize that tradition in a way that would make it come alive in American intellectual circles. He thought the ideals of Catholic educators were satisfactory, but as far as actual practice was concerned, he said, "I find it necessary to level against you a scandalous accusation." He then went on:

> In my opinion . . . you have imitated the worst features of secular education and ignored most of the good ones. There are some good ones, relatively speaking—high academic standards, development of habits of work, and research. . . .

Hutchins listed the bad features he had in mind as athleticism, collegiatism, vocationalism, and anti-intellectualism. In regard to the first two we can claim, I think, that in recent years Catholic institutions have shown improvement, just as all other educational groups have done. As for the second two, vocationalism and anti-intellectualism, I find no striking evidence of reform in the Church's colleges and universities since 1937. Regarding the three good features of secular institutions which Hutchins named, high academic standards, development of habits of work, and the ideal of research, I would say that a better showing has been made here and there on the first, but in the development of habits of work and a cherished ideal of research, I cannot personally see much by way of a fundamental change.

A second major defect in Catholic higher education that helps to account for its paucity of scholars of distinction, is what I would call our betrayal of one another. By that I mean the development within the last two decades of numerous and competing graduate schools, none of which is adequately endowed, and few of which have the trained personnel, the equipment in libraries and laboratories, and the professional wage scales to warrant their ambitious undertakings. The result is a perpetuation of mediocrity and the draining away from each other of the strength that is necessary if really superior achievements are to be attained. . . .

An additional point which should find place in an investigation of this kind is the absence of a love of scholarship for its own sake among American Catholics, and that even among too large a number of Catholics who are engaged in higher education. It might be described as the absence of a sense of dedication to an intellectual apostolate. This defect, in turn, tends to deprive many of those who spend their lives in the universities of the American Church of the admirable industry and unremitting labor in research and publication which characterize a far greater proportion of their colleagues on the faculties of the secular universities. I do not pretend to know precisely what the cause of this may be, but I wonder if it is not in part due to the too literal interpretation which many churchmen and superiors of seminaries and religious houses have given to St. Paul's oft-quoted statement that "Here we have no permanent city, but we seek for the city that is to come," and their emphasis on the question of the author of the *Imitation of Christ* when he asked, "What doth it avail thee to discourse profoundly of the Trinity, if thou be void of humility, and consequently displeasing to the Trinity?" Too frequently, perhaps, those training in our institutions have had the same author's famous dictum, "I had rather feel compunction than know its definition," quoted to them without a counterbalancing emphasis on the evils of intellectual sloth. . . .

Closely connected with the question of the prevailing Catholic attitudes in education is the overemphasis which some authorities of the Church's educational system in the United States have given to the school as an agency for moral development, with an insufficient stress on the role of the school as an instrument for fostering intellectual excellence. That fact has at times led to a confusion of aims and to a neglect of the school as a training ground for the intellectual virtues. No sensible person will for a moment question that the inculcation of moral virtue is one of the principal reasons for having Catholic schools in any circumstances. But that goal should never be permitted to overshadow the fact that the school, at whatever level one may consider it, must maintain a strong emphasis on the cultivation of intellectual excellence. Given superior minds, out of the striving for the intellectual virtues there will flow, with its attendant religious instruction, the formation of a type of student who will not only be able to withstand the strains which life will inevitably force upon his religious faith, but one who will have been so intellectually fortified that he will reflect distinction upon the system of which he is a product.*

• • •

In conclusion, then, one may say that it has been a combination of all the major points made in this paper, along with others which I may have failed to consider, that has produced in American Catholics generally, as well as in the intellectuals, a pervading spirit of separatism from their fellow citizens of other religious faiths. They have suffered from the timidity that characterizes minority groups, from the effects of a ghetto they have themselves fostered, and, too, from a sense of inferiority induced by their consciousness of the inadequacy of Catholic scholarship. But who, one may rightly ask, has been responsible in the main for its inadequacy? Certainly not the Church's enemies, for if one were to reason on that basis St. Augustine would never have written the *City of God,* St. Robert Bellarmine the *Tractatus de potestate summi pontificis,* nor would Cardinal Baronius have produced the *Annales ecclesiastici.* In fact, it has been enmity and opposition that have called forth some of the greatest monuments to Catholic scholarship. The major defect, therefore, lies elsewhere than with the unfriendly attitude of some of those outside the Church. The chief blame, I firmly believe, lies with Catholics themselves. It lies in their frequently self-imposed ghetto mentality which prevents them from mingling as they should with their non-Catholic colleagues, and in their lack of industry and the habits of work, to which Hutchins alluded in 1937. It lies in their failure to have measured up to their responsibilities to the incomparable tradition of Catholic learning of which they are the direct heirs, a failure which Peter Viereck noted, and which suggested to him the caustic question, "Is the honorable adjective 'Roman Catholic' truly merited by America's middleclass-Jansenist Catholicism, puritanized, Calvinized, and dehydrated . . . ?" When the inescapable and exacting labor of true scholarship is intelligently directed

---

* At this point in his original article, Msgr. Ellis gave an extensive review of the evidence of meagre Catholic contributions to American cultural, intellectual, and scientific life. [Editor's note]

and competently expressed it will win its way on its own merits into channels of influence beyond the Catholic pale. Of that one can be certain. . . .

Yet an effective result of this kind is only attained through unremitting labor, prolonged thought, and a sense of the exalted mission of the intellectual apostolate on the part of the Catholic scholar. It was that ideal that Newman kept before him during his famous lectures on the position of the English Catholics at the Birmingham Oratory in the summer of 1851. He challenged his hearers to be equal to the obligation they owed to their non-Catholic fellow-countrymen. As he said:

> They must be made to know us as we are; they must be made to know our religion as it is, not as they fancy it; they must be made to look at us, and they are overcome. This is the work that lies before you in your place and in your measure.

There is not a man of discernment anywhere today who is unaware that the intellectual climate of the United States is undergoing a radical change from the moribund philosophy of materialism and discredited liberalism that have ruled a good portion of the American mind for the better part of a century. Clinton Rossiter spoke of this in a thoughtful article published some months ago. He foresees a new day dawning for our country when religious and moral values will again be found in the honored place they once occupied. Concerning that ray of hope upon the horizon, he concluded: "And it will rest its own strong faith in liberty and constitutional democracy on the bedrock of these traditional, indeed eternal values: religion, justice, morality." If this prediction should prove true, and there is increasing support for the view that it will, to whom, one may ask, may the leaders of the coming generation turn with more rightful expectancy in their search for enlightenment and guidance in the realm of religion and morality than to the American Catholic intellectuals? For it is they who are in possession of the oldest, wisest, and most sublime tradition of learning that the world has ever known. There has, indeed, been considerable improvement among American Catholics in the realm of intellectual affairs in the last half-century, but the need for far more energetic strides is urgent if the receptive attitude of contemporary thought is to be capitalized upon as it should be. It is, therefore, a unique opportunity that lies before the Catholic scholars of the United States which, if approached and executed with the deep conviction of its vital importance for the future of the American Church, may inspire them to do great things and, at the end, to feel that they have in some small measure lived up to the ideal expressed by Père Sertillanges when he said of the Catholic intellectuals:

They, more than others, must be men consecrated by their vocation. . . . The special asceticism and the heroic virtue of the intellectual worker must be their daily portion. But if they consent to this double self-offering, I tell them in the name of the God of Truth not to lose courage.

The Crisis of Americanization

PHILIP GLEASON

Pope John's *aggiornamento* and the Second Vatican Council set the whole Catholic world into ferment; in few areas has the turbulence of change been so severe as in the American Church. The concluding selection in this volume focuses directly on these most recent developments and relates them to the theme of Americanization that has figured either explicitly or implicitly in all of the foregoing essays.

TRANSITION IS TOO MILD A WORD FOR WHAT IS GOING ON IN THE Catholic Church in the United States today. Every day we hear more and more of crises—the crisis in vocations, the crisis of authority, the crisis of faith, and of course the identity crisis. So great is the turbulence of change that hints of uneasiness escape even from those in the forefront of reform. The editor of a journal with the bold title, *Front Line*, remarked not long ago on the danger that the baby might be sent flying out with the bath water, and Michael Novak has pondered the question whether we are witnessing the renewal of Christianity or its slow abandonment. Those of less sanguine temperament might understandably be put in mind of Oliver Wendell Holmes' "wonderful one-hoss shay"; for in describing the vehicle that ran perfectly for a hundred years and then fell apart without warning, Holmes was commenting on the collapse of New England Calvinism a century ago.

The dramatic shifts in American Catholicism can be analyzed from any number of perspectives, each yielding its own insights. To one who has worked in the history of Catholic immigration and learned something of the way immigrant institutions adjusted themselves to the American environment, it seems worthwhile to approach the subject in terms of assimilation or Americanization. Ths approach does not exhaust the possibilities and it may seem to slight the importance of influences from abroad. But if *aggiornamento* is fundamentally an effort to bring the Church into meaningful contact with the modern world, then for Catholics living in the United States it is surely the modern world in its American form that is of primary importance, and one of our most pressing needs is to understand the relationships between Catholicism and American society and culture.

The expression "crisis of Americanization" may be new, but it is common knowledge that the Church in the United States has been profoundly molded by the processes of immigration and acculturation. Over a decade ago, Will Herberg's *Protestant-Catholic-Jew* stressed the importance of immigration in understanding religious phenomena and underscored the complexity of their mutual interrelationships. More recently, Andrew M. Greeley organized his sociological investigation of American Catholic history around the theme of Americanization. The very familiarity of the cliché, "emergence from the ghetto," bespeaks widespread popular recognition that some sort of assimilation has played a major role in reshaping American Catholicism in the past few years. But while everybody says that the Church has recently come out of its ghetto—or that it should do so without delay—it is not really very clear what it means to emerge from a ghetto. Our first task, therefore, is to try to put some substance into this expression by examining just how the processes of assimilation operated with immigrant groups. Having done this, we can apply the findings in an analysis of the transitions of American Catholicism.

THE AMERICANIZATION MODEL

The terms are often used rather loosely, but in general "assimilation" or "Americanization" are understood as designating the processes by which individuals and identifiable social groups shed the characteristics that mark them as foreign, adopt the cultural norms of American society, become fully integrated into American life, and come to think of themselves simply as Americans. Assimilation, in other words, is a collective name for all the innumerable changes immigrants must make in order to get along in American society—changes in the way they act, talk, and think; changes in the pattern of their interaction with others; changes in the conceptions they have of themselves. These changes take place over a long period of time and relatively few persons who immigrate as adults become "fully Americanized." However, it is axiomatic with students of immigration that the American-born children and grandchildren of immigrants—the second and third generations—absorb American ways more completely and are therefore more fully assimilated.

The typical immigrant is not a solitary individual but a member of one or another ethnic, or nationality, group. These groups, made up of persons from the same homeland and sharing the same language and traditions, are held together by a common consciousness of kinship and are given formal structure by a network of institutions such as churches, schools, newspapers, and various kinds of voluntary associations. Assimilation may be thought of as operating on this group level as well as on the individual level. That is, the changes in habits, attitudes, and values among the individual immigrants—especially in the second and later generations—necessarily affect the group of which they constitute the membership and require corresponding adjustments in the institutions which hold the group together and give it form. Assimilation on the level of the organized group takes place more slowly than, and in response to, assimilation on the individual level, but once it has taken place it sets a sort of official seal on the degree of adjustment that has been made.

The "language question," a perennial issue among non-English-speaking groups, provides a good illustration of the relationship between assimilation on these two levels. As more individual immigrants adopt the English language, institutions of the group such as its press and organizations must gradually make room for English or they will eventually wither and die. The linguistic transition often arouses passionate resistance and bitter disagreement, especially between spokesmen for older and younger generations, but when it has been completed, the language shift constitutes an important reformulation of the modality of ethnic loyalty. If an organization of German immigrants, for example, adopts English in its meetings and printed records, the shift amounts to a kind of official group recognition of the legitimacy of a new way of "being German."

What had formerly been thought of as essential to the identity and maintenance of the group—use of the mother tongue—is now designated as accidental. Spokesmen for the group then argue that the "German character" endures in spite of the language change and that those of German descent have an obligation to preserve it and to support the institutions created by earlier generations of immigrants.

Such an adjustment is absolutely indispensable because the institutions of the group are doomed to extinction if they do not keep pace with the Americanization of their clientele. But the need to keep pace with Americanization presents enormous difficulties both for discovering what adjustments are needed and for successfully effecting those deemed appropriate. For one thing, it becomes increasingly perplexing to identify the essence of the group's heritage, as language and other concrete attributes of its traditional culture disappear. If assimilation on the individual level proceeds to the point where persons of a certain national descent abandon all their distinctive cultural characteristics, mix indiscriminately with Americans of other backgrounds, and lose all their ethnic consciousness, they are obviously no longer set apart from others in American society by reason of their ethnic heritage. In other words, they are no longer a group of their own. And when the group has been dissipated in this fashion, the institutions which served it can no longer continue on the old basis. They must either go out of business or justify themselves on the basis of some entirely different rationale, making no claims for support in the name of the heritage they formerly embodied and symbolized.

This hypothetically ultimate stage of assimilation is seldom or perhaps never reached, for a lingering sense of ethnic identity is a very persistent phenomenon. A few ethnic organizations may be able to keep going long after the group seems to have disappeared if there remains a remnant of ethnically conscious persons to support them. But let us take the case of a group at an earlier stage in the process of Americanization—a group still clearly recognizable as such, but one whose membership is rapidly becoming assimilated. The institutions serving such a group confront a dilemma: They must accommodate to the changes in their clientele; yet in doing so they must avoid betraying their heritage, for the preservation of that heritage is the fundamental purpose of their existence and the surest ground of their appeal.

A group in these circumstances must tread a narrow and precarious path between the opposing perils of self-isolation and total absorption. Through its institutions, it must find a way of preserving an inherited distinctiveness in American society without rigidly clinging to the past, cutting itself off from society, and becoming irrelevant to the concerns of its more assimilated constituency. On the other hand, the effort to appeal to its more Americanized members by becoming more actively involved in the "mainstream" of society will be self-defeating unless the peculiar heritage and identity of the group is preserved in some new formulation.

The group cannot afford to remain in a ghetto, to use the popular metaphor, but it cannot afford to come out either if emergence from the ghetto will lead to its dispersal, absorption, and disappearance as a group. There is another currently popular expression which could also be legitimately applied to a group caught in this predicament. It is undergoing an identity crisis—a climactic turning point in its development that requires it to resolve the contradiction of being different from what it was in the past, and yet the same. The fact that both of these expressions have become commonplace in the discussion of contemporary American Catholicism suggests that there is a fundamental analogy between what is going on in the Church and the general processes of immigrant assimilation. There are, of course, important differences between the Church and what we usually think of as an ethnic group. It is also true that the foregoing sketch is quite schematic and overlooks a multitude of factors that have conditioned the development of the various ethnic groups in the United States. But treating assimilation in this abstract fashion highlights some of the crucial features of the process and throws the central dilemma it posed for immigrant groups into sharp relief. This brief review, therefore, furnishes a "model" of the process of Americanization which can be fruitfully applied to an analysis of the present ferment in American Catholicism.

• • •

ASSIMILATION ON THE GROUP LEVEL

Changes in the attitudes and beliefs of the more assimilated younger Catholics are bringing about changes in Catholic institutions just as immigrant organizations had to modify their original structures and programs to keep pace with the Americanization of their clientele. Recent developments among Catholic professional associations provide perhaps the clearest illustration of this sort of Americanization at the group level.

Catholic professional associations have performed a function closely analogous to that of ethnic societies. Voluntary associations of immigrants came into being because people sharing a common background and common values saw that they could not fit comfortably into organizations already existing in American society. These ethnic organizations not only served as congenial settings for sociability and as agencies of mutual support; they also made it possible for those who had a sense of their "peoplehood" (to use Milton M. Gordon's term) to take part as an organized group in the life of the local and national community. Ethnic associations therefore functioned both as institutional symbols of the immigrants' consciousness of their peculiar heritage and character and as organizational vehicles for their participation in American life. But as assimilation eroded the distinctive consciousness of the immigrants and permitted them to mix more freely in the larger society, ethnic organizations were hard put to keep going because the needs that brought them into being were no longer operative.

The case with Catholic professional associations is very similar. They are a new form of Catholic organizational activity. The oldest one of any importance, the National Catholic Educational Association, dates back only to 1904, and an offshoot in the same general area, the National Catholic Guidance Conference, was organized as recently as 1962. Catholic professional associations are clearly a result of the professionalization of nearly all spheres of activity in a highly complex, urban industrial society. Those who set up these organizations were no doubt the first generation of Catholics to be involved in these various spheres of activity after they became professionalized in American society at large. Metaphorically, the founders were the first Catholic "immigrants" to these professional worlds. The organizations they created correspond to ethnic societies in at least three aspects. First, they were designed to improve the performance of activities carried on by, and in the service of, a specific social group. Second, this social group was set apart from other Americans by reason of its heritage, which was regarded as affecting the mode of the group's thinking, the position it should take, and the approach it should follow in whatever professional field was involved. Finally, the associations themselves served as vehicles for Catholics to participate in professional activities and communicate with others in the field on an organized basis, especially through the publication of a professional journal.

If Catholic professional associations perform functions analogous to those of immigrant societies, the question arises: Will they face the same problems as their membership becomes more Americanized? The answer is that some already have, and others seem to be nearing that stage. There has been criticism for some time of such Catholic "ghetto" societies. The remark of a recent Fordham graduate that he remembers "laughing and crying at the same time" when he first heard of "an outfit called the Catholic Poetry Society of America" is typical of the attitude of Catholic liberals. But it is even more significant that members of these professional organizations are themselves asking whether there is any justification for their perpetuation. Thus the *Linacre Quarterly* recently carried an article entitled, "The Catholic Physician's Guild—Do We Really Need One?" A writer in the *Catholic Library World* for April, 1967, felt constrained to offer a vigorous defense for the existence of the Catholic Library Association. And only five years after the American Catholic Psychological Association began to publish a professional journal it printed an article calling upon the society to go out of business because it "represents a divisive, sectarian, ghetto mentality on the American scene."

Skepticism about the desirability of such societies has been heightened by the postconciliar winds of change, but the example of the identity crisis among Catholic sociologists indicates that the roots of the phenomenon are to be sought in processes indigenous to the American scene. It also furnishes some particularly apt comparisons with the experience of ethnic societies.

The study of sociology in Catholic institutions emerged from a matrix of concern over social problems and reform, and the earliest ventures into the field were by persons primarily interested in social work, social ethics, or moral theology. The prehistory of sociology in non-Catholic universities was generally similar, but it established itself as an autonomous discipline around the turn of the century. Those who founded the American Catholic Sociological Society in 1938 belonged to the first generation of Catholic workers in the field who understood sociology as a subject distinct in itself, separate from philosophy or theology, which had its own proper object and methodology.

But while the first generation of professional Catholic sociologists regarded their discipline as a science, they held that it was "not in the full sense of the word an exact science" because the values espoused by the investigator—his ideological stance or philosophy of life—inevitably colored his approach and the inferences he drew from his data. Sociology as it was carried on by non-Catholics was not fully acceptable because, although it claimed to be clinically neutral and to exclude considerations of value, it was really based on naturalistic assumptions that were viewed as being an integral part of the scientific method itself. In these circumstances Catholic sociologists felt that their position was denied a hearing in the existing professional organizations. They believed that by establishing their own society they could not only work more effectively to improve the teaching of socioolgy in Catholic schools, but could also provide a forum in which sociological investigations carried on within the framework of Catholic beliefs and values might be brought before the public.

The American Catholic Sociological Society thus began its career thirty years ago with the explicit determination to erect a "Catholic sociology" combining scientific methodology with the value system derived from religion. By the 1950's, however, there was growing dissatisfaction with this approach among the society's members. There was demand for greater scholarly competence—in keeping with the prevailing self-criticism of Catholic intellectual life in those years—and there was also some complaint about the unprofessional management and familial type of control exercised by the group's leaders. Two other factors are of special interest here which illustrate the trends of assimilation and social acceptance at work generally by mid-century. First, more young Catholics entered the society who had been trained in the leading secular graduate schools or in Catholic universities where sociology had become a fairly autonomous discipline, pursued in up-to-date fashion. These men had absorbed the viewpoint and approach characteristic of their specialty, and they chafed at what they considered the narrow and self-isolating stance of the organization. Second, the younger men could point out that sociology was no longer dominated by the uncritical acceptance of naturalistic assumptions. There was increasingly wide recognition of the important role played by values in sociological investigation; hence Catholics were not automatically barred from gaining recognition in the profession simply because they operated within a religiously derived value system. Moreover, it was sometimes asserted, the values of Catholics did not differ importantly from those of other scholars in their implications for sociological study. For these reasons, the dissidents felt that a Catholic sociological society on the old basis was no longer justified, and they rejected the notion that there could be such a thing as "Catholic sociology." Rather, sociology had to be pursued as a fully autonomous discipline, with each scholar applying normative criteria worked out from a personal synthesis of his own fundamental philosophical or religious beliefs and his professional knowledge.

By 1961, discontent arising from these sources led to the replacement of Executive Secretary Ralph Gallagher, S.J., who had been the principal founder of the organization and a leading exponent of "Catholic sociology." Those who championed a more autonomous professional approach were then free to reshape the Catholic Sociological Society in keeping with their views. Although some felt it should disband, what actually occurred was a reorientation of its activity and goals. At a meeting in 1963, the members voted to change the name of their organ from *American Catholic Sociological Review* to *Sociological Analysis* and to make it a journal specializing in the sociology of religion. An introductory statement in the first issue of the rechristened journal indicated that the change was the evolutionary result of two developments. First, the realization that Catholic sociologists found their proper professional lodgment in organizations differentiated according to their specialized interests rather than n a society organized on the basis of religion alone. Second, the recognition that the sociology of religion was an area of common concern to many members of the society and thus offered the most satisfactory rationale for its existence as a scholarly association. The name *Sociological Analysis* was chosen to avoid giving the impression that it was "a parochial journal" or one whose pages would present "a distinctly 'Catholic sociology.'"

Catholic sociologists naturally have a sophisticated awareness of the identity crisis through which their organization is passing. It is quite possible that the forces unleased by the Council will carry the transformation of the society even further, but it should be emphasized that the identity crisis itself took place earlier than, and independent of, Vatican II. So far, the society has weathered the crisis fairly well. By making the study of the sociology of religion its *raison d'être*, it has formulated a new identity which incorporates meaningful links with the past while at the same time justifying its existence on strictly professional grounds. This evolution in the American Catholic Sociological Society is strikingly similar to the experience of certain ethnic societies. It was brought on by the assimilation of the society's individual members in the surrounding American milieu (in this case, the milieu of academic sociology in the United States), and by their gradual loss of the conviction that their heritage entailed an intellectual standpoint different from that of those outside the group. These internal changes, combined with declining external hostility, required the society to find a new rationale—one that maintains some continuity with the organization's distinctive heritage, but at the same time appeals to the interests of its more assimilated members.

This thumbnail history reveals that Americanization involves a basic intellectual reorientation as well as social and institutional shifts. The same fact is demonstrated even more clearly in the case of the American Catholic Philosophical Association. The identity crisis of the philosophers is not as far advanced as that of the sociologists, and it has been more strongly nfluenced by the general reorientation of Catholic thinking brought on by the Council. Moreover, the teaching of philosophy in Catholic institutions has always been, and continues to be, more intimately related to European currents of thought than is the case with other academic disciplines. (Twenty-five per cent of the Ph.D.'s teaching philosophy in Catholic colleges earned their degrees in Europe, as compared to less than 10 per cent of those teaching in other American schools.) Yet the Catholic philosophers are moving appreciably closer to their counterparts in secular universities in the pluralism that is gaining ground among them. And the existence of an identity crisis is confirmed by the title of the presidential address delivered before their society in 1967: "Who Are We?"

• • •

Ideological shifts and redefinitions in self-conception like those traced in these two professional associations may be discerned almost everywhere on the American Catholic scene. Just as the American-born descendants of immigrants tended to depart from traditional patterns and take their ideas and values from their social milieu, Catholics today are orienting themselves to new reference groups and taking their values from new sources. This sort of Americanization may take puzzling or paradoxical turns—as when Catholics adopt the current anti-Americanism of the Left—but basically it reflects the acceptance by Catholics of the norms of whatever segment of American society they feel closest to by reason of social and educational background, status aspiration, political preference, or ideological persuasion. The editors of *Commonweal,* for example, were disturbed that non-Catholics whom they respected criticized the magazine's stand on abortion. One of them, Daniel Callahan, had earlier made the point, in connection with the theme of honesty, that as soon as an idea gains currency among Protestants it is very shortly taken up by Catholics. The hidden spring of new currents of thought among both Protestants and Catholics, according to Callahan, is "the contemporary world," which is reshaping the consciousness of modern man.

Although the influence of the world upon the Church is anything but new, the effects of that influence are perhaps more far reaching and deeper now than at any earlier moment in the history of American Catholicism. Institutions that seemed immune to change—such as religious communities—feel the shock waves, and a general crisis of identity leaves Catholics wondering who they are, what makes them what they are, and which way they are going. An examination of the controversy over Catholic intellectual life offers one way of approaching the contemporary crisis of confidence.

THE COURSE OF THE CATHOLIC
INTELLECTUALISM DEBATE

It is quite obvious that the Catholic-intellectualism discussion runs parallel to, and was no doubt influenced by, the same sort of discussion in American society at large. The evils of anti-intellectualism and "mass culture" were staples of highbrow journalism in the 1950's when the Catholic controversy got under way in earnest. Now that the center of interest has shifted to issues of higher education, there is again a close correlation between the special Catholic concern and the prevailing American preoccupation with the problems of the multiversity, student unrest, the dissenting academy, and so on. But while it was only a subspecies of the larger phenomenon, the intellectualism controversy had a special significance for Catholics and may be understood as the first major phase of the transformation of American Catholicism that is still in progress.

The beginning of the great debate may be dated from the fall of 1955, when John Tracy Ellis' "American Catholics and the Intellectual Life" was published in *Thought*. This thirty-seven page essay, which was reprinted in book form the following year, provoked a greater reaction than any other piece of comparable length in the history of American Catholicism. A collection of readings—*American Catholicism and the Intellectual Ideal,* compiled by Frank L. Christ and Gerard E. Sherry— contains excerpts from forty-six books and articles appearing between 1955 and 1958. But while Ellis' article provided the spark for the explosion of critical writing, Catholics were far from unconcerned before 1955. Christ and Sherry's collection contains treatments of the subject that go back a century; more than two-thirds of their selections appeared before the publication of Ellis' essay. It was only in the 1950's, however, that assimilation had brought the Catholic community to the point where its intellectual status and prestige was a matter of sufficiently wide interest to become the central issue in American Catholic life. A problem that previously seemed pressing to only a minority now occupied the attention of all thinking Catholics.

The controversy eventually took a turn that really was new, but it also included several themes that had already become standard. Three of these —the leadership theme, the prestige theme, and the missionary theme (to give them names)—share the basically apologetical orientation that had dominated earlier discussions. Although writers who stressed these themes no doubt appreciated the intrinsic value of intellectual activity, they focused principally on the role of intellectual work and achievement in advancing the mission and standing of the Church. In emphasizing the instrumental values of education, scholarship, and intellectual accomplishments, these Catholic writers were adopting the same position taken by spokesmen for immigrant groups. For these groups also realized they needed an elite who could provide leadership, and they developed schools, colleges, and various types of scholarship programs to help produce such an elite.

• • •

The traditional leadership, prestige, and missionary themes persisted in the 1950's, but the discussion soon moved beyond them. The effort to uncover the reasons for the lamentable intellectual record of Catholics and their failure to exert an influence on American culture proportionate to their numbers led to a much more searching critique. When "the real culprit," in Daniel Callahan's words, was identified as "the American Catholic mentality," it followed that improvements in the intellectual sphere could be achieved only by basic changes in the patterns of Catholic life and thought.

But while the controversy broadened out to include practically all facets of Catholic life, the state of intellectual endeavor and the quality of Catholic schools remained important focal points. It was in the context of debate on these matters that a number of general weaknesses were first subjected to heavy criticism. Thus, in calling attention to the unfortunate effects of formalism, authoritarianism, clericalism, moralism, and defensiveness, Thomas F. O'Dea described these attitudes as "the basic characteristics of the American Catholic milieu which inhibit the development of mature intellectual activity. . . ." On this account, those who committed themselves to a radical reordering of Catholic attitudes and values acquired a vested polemical interest in the finding that Catholics were anti-intellectual and that their schools were inferior. Since the woeful condition of Catholic intellectualism confirmed the need for drastic change, improvements in the intellectual sphere could hardly be admitted before drastic change was accomplished. This consideration makes more understandable the otherwise puzzling fact that some "self-critics" were quite reluctant to accept research that indicated a noticeable amelioration of Catholic intellectual life. Likewise, the sociological explanation of Catholic inferiority did not commend itself to some, because if immigrant background and lower-class status were primarily responsible, the situation could be expected to correct itself in time and the need for a purposefully executed reconstruction of Catholic life would be lessened.

The reaction to Andrew M. Greeley's investigation of the career plans of Catholic college graduates is very suggestive in this connection. Although the failure of proportionate numbers to enter upon graduate studies had previously been offered as evidence of Catholic intellectual backwardness, Greeley's finding that Catholics were adequately represented in graduate schools in the 1960's was dismissed by some as irrelevant to the question of Catholic anti-intellectualism. Thus, John D. Donovan argued that the subjects of Greeley's study probably lacked the "free-wheeling, critical, creative, and speculative bent of mind that marks the intellectual," being instead merely "'intelligent' graduates of the collegiate population." And James W. Trent implied that these young people would be "authoritarian, intellectually docile graduate student[s]" who would "contribute little more to the flow of intellectuality and creativity than the ordinary high-school graduate."

These objections highlight a fundamental ambiguity that runs all through the discussion. The nub of the difficulty is: What do terms like "intellectual," "intellectualism," and "anti-intellectualism" really mean? Not only is there no universal agreement on these, but the vagueness of the terminology is such that it is frequently impossible even to specify the points of disagreement. Donovan and Trent seem to think that the term intellectual should be reserved to persons who engage more or less habitually in a certain restricted variety of mental operations. According to this view, the Catholic-intellectualism problem cannot be overcome until there are considerably more Catholics who engage in this sort of mental activity. Greeley, on the other hand, accepts the fact that more Catholics are pursuing postgraduate degrees and planning careers in scholarship as evidence of improvement in Catholic intellectual life. His position assumes that graduate work and professorial careers necessarily involve intellectualism, without any need to establish the freewheeling, critical, creative, and speculative qualities of mind that Donovan and Trent would insist on.

While concepts like intellectualism and anti-intellectualism remain nebulous, there has been a significant development since the controversy began in the 1950's. In its early phases, most writers accepted the premise that although Catholics had made a poor showing as scholars and scientists they could do better simply by trying harder; no inherent incompatibility was posited between being Catholic and being an intellectual. As the controversy waxed, however, more and more Catholic attitudes and patterns of thought and life were listed as obstacles to intellectualism. In order to make a real intellectual breakthrough, it appeared that many things traditionally associated with Catholicism would have to be eliminated. This trend culminated in the affirmation that prior commitment to a dogmatic religious position could not be reconciled with "love of in-tellectuality for its own sake." In other words, true intellectualism was defined in such a way as to exclude religious commitment. Insofar as he was to operate as an intellectual, the Catholic would have to set aside his doctrinal beliefs. The notion that a man might legitimately employ his intellect—as an intellectual—to explicate or defend the Church's position was rejected by Edward Wakin and Joseph F. Scheuer in their book dealing with the "de-Romanization" of American Catholicism. The expression "intellectual apostolate," they wrote, is "a contradiction in terms"; the exhortation to Catholics to take it up "threatens to subvert the intellectual and turn him into a holy panderer for the Catholic Church."

What has happened in the last fifteen years, therefore, is that a campaign which was intended to increase the number of Catholic intellectuals has reached the point of denying that there can be such a thing as a Catholic intellectual. Not everyone who writes on the subject accepts this conclusion; indeed, the conclusion has not even been spelled out in its fullest rigor, although it is logically entailed in the line of reasoning adopted by Wakin and Scheuer. It also corresponds to the progression we have already traced in connection with "Catholic sociology" and to the analogous conclusion that there can be no such thing as a Catholic university.

The performance of the Catholic university has always occupied an important place in the controversy. The question of scholarship is intrinsic to the university, and most of the other matters touched on in the debate —the role of the layman, clericalism, paternalism, social divisiveness, and so on—have a bearing on the functioning of Catholic colleges and universities. Moreover, the faculty and students in Catholic institutions of higher education constitute an increasingly large and articulate group with a personal interest in the outcome of the controversy. For all these reasons, which have been dramatized by several spectacular eruptions over academic freedom, the discussion of Catholic intellectual life has tended in the last few years to become a discussion of Catholic higher education.

As the debate has evolved along these lines, Catholic higher education itself has been reshaped by a number of changes. Enrollments have more than doubled since World War II; the social and educational background of students is much higher than in previous generations; lay faculties have grown and have better professional preparation; graduate schools dedicated to research now set the tone in the better institutions; new patterns of administration and policy-making have been introduced looking to the reduction, or elimination, of control by nonacademic religious authorities. These changes have brought about a marked improvement in the academic quality of Catholic higher education. They have also had the effect of making Catholic colleges, and especially universities, more like other American institutions of higher learning. The combined result of improved quality and closer approximation of secular norms has been to raise the question: What is it that is specifically Catholic about Catholic colleges and universities? Bernard Shaw's dictum that a Catholic university is a contradiction in terms has been invoked to the point of tedium; John Cogley, to whom the Catholic university is as outmoded as the Papal States, has rewritten Gertrude Stein in insisting that a university is a university is a university. Contrary to the expectation of many who called for improvements, upgrading the Catholic university has not solved the problem; rather it has uncovered the deeper problem of whether there is any justification for a Catholic university regardless of how good it might be.

If this is an identity crisis, it is equally a crisis of assimilation. In the case of immigrants, it was precisely the identity of the group that was at stake in the process of assimilation. Like the spokesmen for immigrant nationalities, the early writers on Catholic intellectual life took it as a given fact that Catholics were a distinctive group with a distinctive outlook on the world. As such, they needed to train leaders who could expound their position and win recognition for it. Leaders were also needed to explain to the members of the group themselves just what their position was, how it might be applied to the problems of life, and where it should be modified in keeping with changing circumstances. Catholic colleges and universities seemed so obviously the appropriate institutions to perform these functions that no one ever thought of challenging them to justify their existence. Earlier generations of Catholics were critical of the weaknesses of their colleges, but they never really doubted that such institutions had a vitally important role to play.

Now, however, assimilation has brought the Catholic population to the point where it differs only marginally from American society at large. Catholic scholars in various disciplines are discarding the belief that their faith dictates an approach different from that of non-Catholic workers in the same fields. Leading Catholic universities have accepted the model of outstanding secular institutions, pledging their readiness to "pay any price, break any mold" in their pursuit of academic excellence. Only a small minority is demanding the outright secularization of Catholic higher education, but the general trend is clearly in that direction. Those still convinced of the value of Catholic higher education and of the need for Catholic universities find themselves increasingly perplexed at the rising clamor of demands that they explain the grounds of their conviction. In the past, the need for Catholic universities was an *assumption*—an assumption that arose from the consciousness on the part of Catholics that they were "different," a distinctive group whose needs could only be met by institutions that corresponded to their own unique character. Now the assimilation of the Catholic population and the acceptance of secular American norms by Catholic scholars and institutions of higher learning have eroded the social reality which made that assumption seem inevitable and right. Those who still believe that Catholic higher education is needed and valuable can no longer regard their belief as a premise of action whose validity is beyond question. Rather, they are required to bring their assumptions up to the level of conscious analysis, explicate them, and demonstrate their validity to the world.

This sort of task is never easy, for what is at issue is a people's basic understanding of who they are and what it is that makes them what they are. But when the experience of a people forces upon them the consciousness that they no longer are what they once were, yet leaves them uncertain as to their present identity, the task can hardly be avoided. Whether American Catholic intellectuals and educators can accomplish the task successfully is still an open question.

THE AMBIGUITIES OF AMERICANIZATION

The developments we have reviewed correspond closely to the Americanization model sketched earlier. Assimilation on the individual level has not only brought Catholics abreast of their fellow citizens in respect to social and economic status, it has also resulted in a new self-conception for those who have increasingly adopted the attitudes and beliefs prevailing in secular society. These changes in the social composition and outlook of the group require a reshaping of Catholic institutions to bring them into line with the shifting configuration of the clientele whose needs they serve and whose values they symbolize and embody. A number of these institutional and ideological changes were already under way before Vatican II, but the loosening of traditional patterns set in motion by the Council has vastly accelerated the general tendency. All the old beliefs and patterns of action are called into question; all the old institutions must justify themselves afresh and demonstrate their relevance to the new situation.

When an immigrant group reached an analogous stage in the process of assimilation, the challenge faced by its institutions—and by the group as a whole—was to find some middle way between the opposing perils of self-isolation and total absorption. Rigid adherence to traditional attitudes and structures condemned the group and its institutions to slow extinction—but unreservedly embracing the norms and values of the dominant culture was tantamount to admitting that the group stood for no values of its own worth preserving, that it had nothing distinctive to bring to the larger culture, that it was prepared to confess its spiritual destitution and submerge itself in the "mainstream" of society.

This is the kind of Americanization crisis that now confronts the Catholic Church in the United States. Far-reaching changes are needed to bring the Church into line with modern society and culture and to accommodate to the new mentality gaining ground among Catholics. But it is cruelly difficult to make such changes while at the same time preserving an underlying continuity with the past, preventing the loss of identity, and maintaining minimal cohesiveness within the Catholic population. One of the principal problems is simply to form an adequate idea of what is happening, and especially to grasp clearly the dialectical relationship of the demands and dangers of a situation in which the Church must maintain identity without isolation and achieve relevance without absorption. To judge from much contemporary talk, the complexities and ambiguities of this situation are not very well understood; unfortunately, the terms in which the discussion is frequently carried on tend to conceal the problem rather than clarify it.

Consider, for example, the metaphor of "the mainstream." Lionel Trilling pointed out some years ago that the expression "main currents in American thought" was misleading because it tended toward monism and obscured the fact that culture is a dialectical process involving confrontation and interchange between differing or opposed ideas and values. Nowadays, the Church is being called upon to plunge into "the mainstream" and make itself "relevant." Presumably it would not become especially relevant if it did nothing more than float with the tide. Yet spokesmen for the mainstream policy have little to say about the distinctive additions the Church might make to the mainstream. Nothing that characterized the Church in its "ghetto" days would seem to be acceptable, and one sometimes gets the impression that these writers are exhorting the Church to "get with it" by conforming itself completely to the prevailing currents of American society. There are similar problems with other popular ways of talking. It is far from clear, for example, what "openness" requires, but it might be interpreted to mean that a Church that is "completely open" has no character of its own and must take its substantive content from sources outside itself. And does it not imply something quite similar to say that the only way for the Church to be Catholic with a capital "C" is to be catholic with a small "c"?

According to a writer in *Concilium,* "There is in fact *no* opposition between what is temporal and what is spiritual and eternal" [emphasis added]. Are we then to conclude that the world in which we find ourselves is sufficient unto itself and that the Church has no unique message to bring to it, no standpoint of its own from which the world can be brought under judgment? If this conclusion were to be accepted, we would have to say that Catholicism emerges from its ghetto with nothing specifically its own to contribute to American society. In that case, the Catholic identity would be nothing but the natural accretion of the history of certain social groups, built up by their common past and sustained by purely temporal institutions that came into being in the ordinary course of human affairs. This sort of Catholic identity would not differ essentially from the Germanness of German immigrants, or the ethnic identity of any other nationality group. It would amount to nothing more than another kind of tribalism. How ironic it would be if American Catholic reformers, who began with the determination to eradicate the vestiges of ethnic tribalism from their Church, found themselves at the end with nothing to cling to but a new kind of tribalism! Yet Rosemary Ruether suggests this line of reasoning when she writes that "the terms 'Protestant' and 'Roman Catholic' should be regarded as statements of our tribal affinity . . . and not statements of our faith."

Few Catholics would be willing to concede that their Church is a tribal affair. On the contrary, the vast majority of American Catholics, as well as the officially constituted authorities of the Church, would insist that it is precisely at this point that the Americanization model derived from the experience of ethnic groups breaks down. For they would maintain that the identity of Catholics *as Catholics* differs essentially from ethnic identity—that the Catholic identity is of an entirely different order from the culturally generated inheritances that define various ethnic groups. It is of a wholly different order because of something at the core of Catholicism that is *not* purely natural, *not* merely the accretion of the human past. That which specifically defines Catholicism comes to the Church from outside history: It is the transcendant element of divinity which entered decisively into human history through the person of Jesus Christ and has remained present to the world in and through the Church. And precisely because this essential element in the Church is transhistorical and transcultural, Catholicism—and hence the Catholic identity— *can* adapt and maintain itself through manifold historical and cultural changes.

But while the essential dimension of Catholicity is transhistorical and transcultural, the Church must embody itself in time through changing human structures and engage itself in the concerns of persons who live in a variety of shifting social and historical situations, persons whose identity as Catholics becomes closely interwoven with historically conditioned ways of acting and ways of conceiving of themselves. So there inevitably arises a tension—which has always been present in the history of the Church—between what the Church is in its fullest ontological reality and what it becomes in the contingencies of historical existence. Both elements in this polarity are necessary; the dialectical tension between them will remain for as long as the Church and the world exist. What American Catholics now find themselves grappling with is their own particular form of the classic problem of Christ and culture or the relationship of the Church to the world.

Situating the "crisis of Americanization" in this context places it in the only perspective from which a solution may be adequately approached. But it also raises theological and ecclesiological problems with which I am not competent to deal. I will therefore conclude with one brief comment on the present situation.

American Catholics are concerned about eliminating from the Church the inappropriate cultural forms of the past and making it relevant to modern problems and the modern mentality. Although this concern is necessary and praiseworthy, it also involves two potential perils. Both are related to the inevitable dialectical tension just discussed. On the one hand, Catholics may be tempted to denigrate and despise their own past. But despite the inadequacies of the past, and despite the incongruities between Catholic traditions and structures and the American environment, those now outmoded institutions and cultural forms did embody the Church, making present to the American world the transcendant reality the Church claims to represent. To forget that fact would be to run the risk of losing hold of the conviction that something of surpassing value has been transmitted to us by our past. On the other hand, to strive with blinkered singlemindedness for relevance to the contemporary runs the risk of forgetting that, while the Church must be engaged in the world, it cannot be completely assimilated to the world. Catholicism has come disastrously close to becoming a culture religion in other times and places; for it to become a culture religion now—even in the name of relevance—would be a religious catastrophe and would contribute nothing to the solution of the problems of society.

SELECTIVE
BIBLIOGRAPHY

The literature on American Catholic history includes many valuable biographies, histories of dioceses, religious communities, and other institutions which cannot be listed here. John Tracy Ellis, *A Guide to American Catholic History* (1959) is the best guide to the whole field. It may be supplemented by Edward Vollmar, *The Catholic Church in America: An Historical Bibliography* (1963) and Aubert J. Clark, "Seventy-Five Years of American Church History," *American Ecclesiastical Review, CLI* (August, 1964). The most inclusive historiographical account is John P. Cadden, *The Historiography of the American Catholic Church: 1785-1943* (1944). John Gilmary Shea's work is brilliantly analyzed by Henry Warner Bowden in *Catholic Historical Review, LIV,* (July, 1968). David J. O'Brien, "American Catholic Historiography: A Post-Conciliar Evaluation," *Church History, XXXVII* (March, 1968) reflects the influence of recent changes in Catholic thought and may be interestingly contrasted with Francis X. Curran, "Some Problems of an Historian of the American Church," *Historical Records and Studies, XLIV* (1956). The ecclesiological problems of church history may be approached through Hubert Jedin's introduction to H. Jedin and J. Dolan, *Handbook of*

Church History, vol. I (1965), and, less directly, through Hans Küng, *The Church* (1968).

Henry J. Browne, who wrote a historiographical article a decade ago (*Church History,* XXVI [December, 1957]), also contributed a brief survey of "Catholicism in the United States" to *The Shaping of American Religion,* edited by J. W. Smith and A. L. Jamison (1961). Longer general accounts are J. T. Ellis, *American Catholicism* (1956) and Thomas T. McAvoy, *History of the Catholic Church in the United States* (1969). Theodore Roemer, *The Catholic Church in the United States* (1950) is textbookish; Theodore Maynard, *The Story of American Catholicism* (1941) is lively but not always reliable. J. T. Ellis, *Documents of American Catholic History* (1956) is a very good collection.

Ellis carried the tradition of episcopal biography to its modern climax in his impressive two-volume *Life of James Cardinal Gibbons* (1952) which is almost encyclopedic for the whole era 1870-1920. A number of Ellis' students at the Catholic University of America also contributed major biographies. Thanks to these biographical studies, to T. T. Mc-Avoy, *The Great Crisis in American Catholic History, 1895-1900* (1957), and to Robert D. Cross, *The Emergence of Liberal Catholicism in America* (1958), the period of the controversy over Americanization in the late nineteenth century is probably the most thoroughly investigated phase of American Catholic history. The scholarly biography of Isaac T. Hecker has not yet reached that aspect of Hecker's career and posthumous reputation, but Vincent F. Holden's first volume, *The Yankee Paul* (1958) is an excellent treatment of the early life of a man who was a key figure in the effort to reconcile Catholicism and Americanism. Much has been written about Hecker's friend and ally, Orestes A. Brownson, but Theodore Maynard, *Orestes Brownson, Yankee, Radical, Catholic* (1943) is the most satisfactory treatment available in one volume.

Daniel F. Reilly, *The School Controversy (1891-1893)* (1943) and Colman J. Barry, *The Catholic Church and German Americans* (1953) are indispensible for the period of controversies, but both education and immigration need more study. For the former, there is no comprehensive study more recent than J. A. Burns and B. F. Kohlbrenner, *A History of Catholic Education in the United States* (1937). Neil G. McCluskey, *Catholic Education in America: A Documentary History* (1964) is useful and McCluskey's recent analysis of the present situation, *Catholic*

Education Faces Its Future (1969) contains a good historical discussion, based in part on T. T. McAvoy's provocative article, "Public Schools vs. Catholic Schools and James McMaster," *Review of Politics, XXVIII* (January, 1966). General accounts of Catholic higher education are Edward J. Power, *A History of Catholic Higher Education in the United States* (1958) and Philip Gleason, "American Catholic Higher Education: A Historical Perspective," in *The Shape of Catholic Higher Education,* ed. by R. Hassenger (1967).

Barry's book on the Germans, which concentrates on the 1880s and 1890s is supplemented by Philip Gleason, *The Conservative Reformers: German-American Catholics and the Social Order* (1968) which covers the years 1900–1930. Vincent J. Fecher, *A Study of the Movement for German National Parishes in Philadelphia and Baltimore (1787-1802)* (1955) is an important monograph on the earliest national parishes and "trusteeism" (resistance on the part of laymen and refractory clerics to constituted ecclesiastical authority). Joseph E. Ciesluk, *National Parishes in the United States* (1944) is inadequate but the only general survey and Patrick J. Dignan, *A History of the Legal Incorporation of Church Property in the United States, 1784-1932* (1933) is old and legalistic in approach but there is nothing better on trusteeism. Mary Gilbert Kelly, *Catholic Immigrant Colonization Projects, 1815-1860* (1939) and James P. Shannon, *Catholic Colonization on the Western Frontier* (1957) are of high quality. Various immigrant groups figure in diocesan histories and the like, but scholarly works on Catholic immigration and assimilation are scarce. Works cited in the footnotes to Nathan Glazer and Daniel P. Moynihan, *Beyond the Melting Pot* (1963) are relevant to the topic, as are these additional titles: William V. Shannon, *The American Irish* (1963); Thomas N. Brown, *Irish-American Nationalism* (1966); P. Gleason, "Immigration and American Catholic Intellectual Life," *Review of Politics, XXVI* (April, 1964); Victor R. Greene, "For God and Country: The Origins of Slavic Catholic Self-Consciousness in America," *Church History, XXXV* (December, 1966); and Rudolph J. Vecoli, "Prelates and Peasants; Italian Immigrants and the Catholic Church," *Journal of Social History, II* (Spring, 1969).

Because anti-Catholicism impinges on political life, books like Ray Allen Billington, *The Protestant Crusade* (1938), John Higham, *Strangers in the Land* (1955), and Donald Kinzer, *An Episode in Anti-*

Catholicism: The American Protective Association (1964) are relevant to Catholic political involvement. For the intolerant 1920s see J. Joseph Huthmacher *Massachusetts People and Politics* (1959) and Oscar Handlin, *Al Smith and His America* (1958); for the 1930s, see George Q. Flynn, *American Catholics and the Roosevelt Presidency, 1932-1936* (1968), Charles J. Tull, *Father Coughlin and the New Deal* (1965), and J. David Valaik, "Catholics, Neutrality, and the Spanish Embargo, 1937-1939," *Journal of American History, LIV,* (June, 1968). Vincent P. DeSantis, "American Catholics and McCarthyism," *Catholic Historical Review, LI* (April, 1965) is a good survey, and Lawrence H. Fuchs, *John F. Kennedy and American Catholicism* (1967) covers the Catholic breakthrough in presidential politics.

Aaron I. Abell, *American Catholicism and Social Action* (1960) synthesizes the story of social Catholicism from 1865 to 1950. Abell's *American Catholic Thought on Social Questions* (1968) is a splendid documentary collection. For the earlier period see C. J. Nuesse, *The Social Thought of American Catholics, 1634-1829* (1945). On Catholics and labor see Wayne Broehl, *The Molly Maguires* (1964), Henry J. Browne, *The Catholic Church and the Knights of Labor* (1949), Victor R. Greene, *The Slavic Community on Strike* (1968), and Marc Karson, *American Labor Unions and Politics, 1900-1918* (1958). For the most important personality in twentieth-century Catholic social action see John A. Ryan's autobiography, *Social Doctrine in Action* (1941) and Francis L. Broderick, *Right Reverend New Dealer* (1963).

Thomas T. McAvoy's articles did much to stimulate interest in the relationship of Catholicism to its American environment. Will Herberg drew upon McAvoy's work in his important *Protestant-Catholic-Jew* (1955) and so did Daniel Callahan in *The Mind of the Catholic Layman* (1963). Deserving of special mention among the many works produced during the Catholic intellectualism debate of the 1950s are Thomas F. O'Dea, *American Catholic Dilemma* (1958) and two books by Walter Ong: *Frontiers of American Catholicism* (1957) and *American Catholic Crossroads* (1959). John Courtney Murray's *We Hold These Truths* (1960) is a fine collection of essays; see also Murray, *The Problem of Religious Freedom* (1965). Thomas O'Brien Hanley, *Their Rights and Liberties* (1959) probes the seventeenth-century Maryland background of the Catholic church-state tradition. Two sociologists have attempted to relate the history of American Catholics to contemporary concerns: Dorothy Dohen, *Nationalism and American Catholicism* (1967) has serious conceptual weaknesses; Andrew M. Greeley, *The Catholic Experience* (1967), historically informed and persuasively argued, is an interpretation of major importance. A very brief discussion by a historian that develops similar points is James Hennesey, "The American Experience of the Roman Catholic Church," *Dialog: A Journal of Theology*, IV (Summer, 1965). Stafford Poole, "Americanizing American Religious Life," *America*, CXX (March 15, 1969), is a prescription for current change based on the national experience.